AUSTR

TRAVEL GUIDE
2023

ROSE SYLVESTER

TABLE OF CONTENTS

INTRODUCTION

Australia, a land of vast horizons and breathtaking beauty, captured my heart and soul during my recent journey. From the moment I stepped foot on this awe-inspiring continent, I was greeted by a sense of adventure and wonder that would accompany me throughout my entire trip. As I reflect on my experiences, I am filled with a profound sense of gratitude for the remarkable moments and unforgettable memories that Australia has gifted me.

The diversity of Australia's landscapes is truly unparalleled. From the sun-kissed beaches that stretch as far as the eye can see, to the ancient rainforests teeming with life, and the rugged Outback that seems to extend into eternity, each destination offered a unique and captivating experience. I found myself standing in awe at the iconic beauty of the Great Barrier Reef, witnessing the kaleidoscope of colors beneath the crystal-clear waters. Snorkeling amongst vibrant coral reefs and swimming alongside majestic marine creatures was a surreal and humbling experience that will forever be etched in my memory.

Venturing into the heart of the Red Centre, I found myself face to face with the majestic Uluru. As the sun dipped below the horizon, the rock seemed to radiate deep and sacred energy, filling me with a profound sense of reverence for the land and its ancient stories. I embarked on a journey of discovery, learning about the rich Aboriginal culture and the spiritual significance of this sacred site. The connection I felt with the land and its people left an indelible mark on my soul, igniting a deep appreciation for the wisdom and resilience of the indigenous communities.

Exploring the vibrant cities of Australia was a captivating experience in itself. Sydney, with its iconic landmarks and buzzing energy, had an infectious spirit that compelled me to wander its lively streets and immerse myself in its cosmopolitan charm. Melbourne, with its thriving arts scene and eclectic laneways, invited me to delve into its creative heart and indulge in its diverse culinary offerings. Each city I visited had its distinct personality, yet they all shared a common thread of warmth and friendliness that made me feel welcome and at home.

But it wasn't just the natural wonders and urban delights that enchanted me; it was the people of Australia who truly left an indelible mark on my journey. The genuine kindness and hospitality of the locals were evident in every interaction. From the warm smiles exchanged with strangers to the heartfelt conversations shared over a meal, I felt a sense of belonging and connection that transcended cultural differences. The stories I heard, the laughter we shared, and the friendships I formed are treasures that I will forever hold dear.

Australia's rich cultural tapestry, influenced by its indigenous heritage and multicultural society, fascinated me at every turn. I delved into the ancient Dreamtime stories, the intricate art forms, and the vibrant festivals that celebrated the country's diverse heritage. The fusion of flavors in the cuisine, from indigenous bush tucker to international delights, awakened my taste buds to new sensations and culinary adventures.

During my journey through Australia, I embarked on a culinary adventure that delighted my taste buds and introduced me to a world of flavors and culinary traditions. From fresh seafood caught along the stunning coastline to hearty pub classics and multicultural fusion, Australia's culinary scene proved to be a gastronomic paradise. Here are some of the culinary delights and drinks that captivated me during my trip, along with the locations where I discovered them.

Sydney's Seafood Extravaganza

- As a coastal city, Sydney boasts a remarkable array of fresh seafood delicacies. I indulged in succulent Sydney rock oysters at the iconic Sydney Fish Market, savoring their briny sweetness as I soaked in the vibrant atmosphere of the bustling market. For a true seafood feast, I ventured to one of the seafood restaurants along the waterfront in Darling Harbour or Circular Quay, where I sampled grilled barramundi, buttery Moreton Bay bugs, and flavorsome prawns straight from the grill.

Melbourne's Café Culture:

- Melbourne's vibrant café culture is renowned worldwide, and I couldn't resist immersing myself in the city's thriving coffee scene. I found myself drawn to the quirky laneways and hidden gems where baristas expertly crafted velvety flat whites and aromatic pour-over coffees. Whether it was in the trendy neighborhoods of Fitzroy and Collingwood or the iconic café-lined streets of Degraves and Hardware Lane, Melbourne's café culture provided a delightful respite as I savored each sip in the company of locals and fellow travelers.

Adelaide's Wine and Food Pairings:

- In South Australia, I ventured to the wine regions in Barossa Valley, where I indulged in wine tastings at world-class wineries, pairing award-winning Shiraz with artisanal cheeses and locally sourced produce. The charming town of McLaren Vale also captured my heart with its boutique wineries and cellar doors, offering a chance to savor elegant Cabernet Sauvignon and rich Grenache, perfectly complemented by regional delights such as handmade chocolates and freshly baked bread.

Brisbane's Urban Food Hubs:

- In Brisbane, I discovered a vibrant food scene centered around bustling markets and urban food hubs. The Eat Street Northshore market, located on the banks of the Brisbane River, enchanted me with its lively atmosphere and abundance of international flavors. From mouthwatering Asian street food to wood-fired pizzas and delectable desserts, I embarked on a culinary journey around the world in one vibrant location. For a taste of local Queensland produce, I visited the Jan

Powers Farmers Markets, where I sampled tropical fruits, artisanal cheeses, and freshly baked pastries.

Perth's Fusion Cuisine:

- Perth surprised me with its innovative culinary scene, blending multicultural influences with fresh local produce. In the trendy neighborhoods of Northbridge and Mount Lawley, I explored a diverse range of eateries offering creative fusion dishes. I relished the flavors of Asian-inspired tapas, tantalizing Middle Eastern mezze, and inventive modern Australian cuisine. The city's thriving small bar scene also offered a chance to sample local craft beers, innovative cocktails, and premium Western Australian wines.

Tasmania's Gourmet Delights:

- No culinary journey through Australia would be complete without a visit to Tasmania. Known for its pristine wilderness and gourmet produce, the island state captivated me with its farm-to-table dining experiences. In Hobart, I dined at award-winning restaurants, indulging in dishes featuring locally sourced ingredients such as succulent Tasmanian salmon, creamy cheeses, and delicate truffles. A visit to the Salamanca Market allowed me to discover artisanal preserves, freshly baked goods, and handcrafted chocolates, perfect for sampling and bringing home as edible souvenirs.

Another thing that also blew my mind away and made my trip unforgettable was that I had the privilege of immersing myself in vibrant cultural festivals, exploring fascinating museums, and visiting top attractions that left an indelible mark on my travel experience. From the celebration of indigenous heritage to contemporary art exhibitions and iconic landmarks, Australia's cultural tapestry unfolded before my eyes, captivating me at every turn. Here are some of

the festivals and museums that captivated me
during my trip.

Festivals Celebrating Australian Culture:

- Australia's calendar is brimming with
  festivals that celebrate its rich cultural
  heritage. The mesmerizing Sydney
  Festival kicked off my journey,
  showcasing a diverse program of music,
  art, dance, and theater against the
  backdrop of the iconic Sydney Opera
  House. I was captivated by the lively
  atmosphere and world-class performances
  that showcased both local and
  international talent. The Adelaide Fringe
  Festival, known for its vibrant street
  performances and unconventional art
  displays, allowed me to immerse myself

in the city's artistic spirit. Additionally, I was fortunate enough to witness the mesmerizing traditional dance and music performances during the Festival of the Winds in Sydney, celebrating the diverse cultures that make up modern Australia.

Museums Showcasing Australia's History and Art:

- Australia's museums offer a captivating glimpse into the country's rich history and artistry. The National Museum of Australia in Canberra presented an immersive journey through the nation's past, allowing me to explore the stories of Australia's indigenous peoples, colonial heritage, and contemporary cultural identity. The Museum of Old and New Art (MONA) in Hobart, Tasmania, stunned me with its thought-provoking exhibitions, showcasing contemporary art, antiquities, and unique installations that pushed the boundaries of artistic expression. Additionally, the Art Gallery of New South Wales in Sydney and the National Gallery of Victoria in Melbourne exhibited world-class collections of Australian and international art, offering a visual feast for art enthusiasts.

It was a journey that awakened my senses, expanded my horizons, and reminded me of the sheer beauty and wonder that exists in the world. The moments of awe-inspiring natural beauty, the connections forged with kindred spirits, and the deep appreciation for the land and its people have left an indelible imprint on my soul. Join me in this travel guide, as I take you on an unforgettable tour of this amazing country!

CHAPTER ONE

WELCOME TO AUSTRALIA

Welcome to Australia, the world's sixth-largest country, and a home of magnificent scenery, distinctive wildlife, and various cultures. Australia is a country that is recognized for its friendly and laid-back people, dynamic cities, clean beaches, and magnificent natural treasures.

This island continent is located in the southern hemisphere, bounded by the Pacific Ocean to the east, the Indian Ocean to the west, and the Southern Ocean to the south.

One of the first things that tourists notice about Australia is its immensity. The country is nearly the same size as the United States, but with a population of just over 25 million people, it is one of the world's most sparsely inhabited countries.

Much of Australia's interior is covered by a large, desert known as the Outback, while the eastern and southeastern coasts are home to lush forests, rolling hills, and fertile farms. Australia's northern coastline is tropical, including rainforests, mangrove swamps, and the Great Barrier Reef.

Australia is also home to some of the world's most unusual and intriguing animals, including kangaroos, koalas, wombats, and Tasmanian devils. Visitors may observe these renowned creatures in wildlife parks, sanctuaries, and zoos around the country. Australia is also a birdwatcher's delight, with over 800 bird species documented throughout the country.

One of the nicest things about Australia is the diversity of its culture. The country has a rich Indigenous heritage that extends back tens of thousands of years, and tourists may learn about the traditions, rituals, and beliefs of Australia's

First Nations people through cultural experiences and excursions. Australia's current culture is a melting pot of influences from all over the world, including Europe, Asia, Africa, and the Middle East. This cultural richness is represented in Australia's food, art, music, and festivals.

Australia is famed for its sunny weather, and while the temperature can vary around the country, it is often warm and dry, particularly in the summer months from December to February.

However, it's crucial to understand that Australia may also suffer extreme weather events, such as bushfires, floods, and tropical cyclones, so tourists should keep educated about any possible threats.

AUSTRALIAN GEOGRAPHY AND CLIMATE

Australia's topography and climate are both distinctive and diverse, and understanding them is vital to planning a successful vacation to this huge nation. Australia is the world's sixth-largest country and occupies a full continent in the southern hemisphere, making it one of the most isolated countries in the world.

The country is split into six states and two territories, each having its unique landscapes, climate, and attractions. The states include New South Wales, Queensland, South Australia, Tasmania, Victoria, and Western Australia, while the territories are the Australian Capital Territory and the Northern Territory.

The most striking element of Australia's landscape is its immensity. The country encompasses an area of over 7.7 million square kilometers, making it the world's biggest island and the only continent that is also a country.

Australia is also the flattest continent in the world, with an average elevation of 330 meters.

The most renowned natural feature in Australia is Uluru, also known as Ayers Rock, located in the Northern Territory. Uluru is a large sandstone rock structure that rises 348 meters over the desert environment and is revered by the native Anangu people. Other prominent natural features include the Great Barrier Reef, the world's biggest coral reef system, and the Blue Mountains, a picturesque mountain range in New South Wales.

Australia's climate is similarly diverse, with various regions experiencing a range of temperatures and weather patterns throughout the year. Generally, Australia's climate may be classified as warm and dry, with scorching summers and moderate winters. However, there are noteworthy outliers, such as the tropical climate of northern Australia and the milder climate of Tasmania.

In the summer months from December to February, temperatures may reach as high as 40°C in some regions of the nation, while in the winter months from June to August, temperatures can plummet to below-freezing locations. The coastal parts of Australia are recognized for their warm and pleasant temperature, whereas the interior of the nation, notably the Outback, may endure intense heat and drought.

Australia is also prone to natural calamities such as bushfires, floods, and tropical cyclones, particularly during the summer months. Visitors should be aware of these dangers and be informed about any potential hazards.

In essence, understanding Australia's geography and climate is vital for arranging a successful vacation to this huge and diverse nation. Visitors should anticipate a diversity of landscapes and weather patterns, from the tropical rainforests of the north to the deserts of the interior, and should be prepared for the distinct challenges that each location brings.

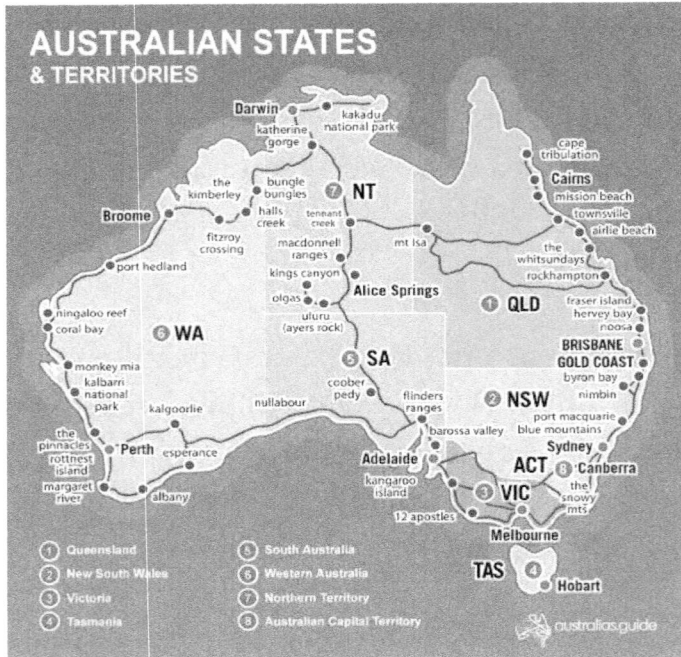

BRIEF HISTORY OF AUSTRALIA

The history of Australia is a complicated and intriguing narrative that stretches back tens of thousands of years. Australia is home to the world's longest continuous civilization, with Indigenous Australians living on the continent for over 60,000 years.

The introduction of European settlers in the late 18th century had a tremendous influence on Indigenous populations and impacted the country's contemporary history.

Indigenous Australians have a rich and diversified culture, with over 500 unique language groups and a profound spiritual connection to the land. They hunted, fished, and collected sustenance from the land, and built sophisticated social structures and systems of government.

The entrance of European settlers in 1788 brought new illnesses, violence, and forced relocation from customary territories, causing tremendous devastation to Indigenous tribes.

In 1770, British explorer Captain James Cook claimed the east coast of Australia for Britain, and in 1788 the First Fleet arrived in Sydney with nearly 1,000 British immigrants, largely convicts.

The British created colonies in other regions of Australia, including Tasmania, Victoria, and Western Australia, and started to advance throughout the continent.

In the early years of British occupation, the colony was controlled by a military government, with Governor Arthur Phillip in command. The colony flourished swiftly, with free settlers coming in increasing numbers and criminals finishing their terms and being released into the community.

In 1851, gold was discovered in Victoria, resulting in a tremendous inflow of migrants and converting the colony into a wealthy and affluent state. Other colonies followed suit, with gold rushes erupting in New South Wales and Western Australia.

In 1901, the colonies united to establish the Commonwealth of Australia, with the new nation ruled under a federal system with powers split between the national government and the states.

The new administration enacted policies of protectionism and immigration restriction, which were aimed to foster economic development and maintain a homogenous population.

Australia engaged in both World War I and World War II, with large deployments of troops and resources. After World War II, Australia saw substantial social and economic transformations, with the post-war boom contributing to increasing wealth and the rise of the welfare state.

In the second part of the 20th century, Australia grew more multicultural, with more migration from non-European nations and rising awareness of Indigenous rights and reconciliation. Today, Australia is a successful and varied nation, with a rich cultural legacy and a dedication to democracy, freedom, and equality.

POLITICS

All the colonies except Western Australia acquired responsible self-government. New South Wales led the way when an imperial statute of 1842 created a two-thirds elective legislature.

The Australian Colonies Government Act (1850) expanded this condition to Victoria, South Australia, and Tasmania. The legislation allowed room for subsequent amendment of the colonial constitutions, and in 1855–56 this took effect in the four colonies, Tasmania thereafter losing the name Van Diemen's Land. Queensland followed its split from New South Wales.

All had bicameral legislatures, with ministers answerable to the lower chambers, which by 1860, save in Tasmania, were elected on a near-democratic basis (all adult non-Aboriginal men were entitled to vote). In Victoria and South Australia, the secret ballot was introduced in 1856 (see Australian ballot).

While the imperial power thus responded to colonial aspirations for self-rule, on the route there were some heated moments. Virtually all colonists abhorred paying taxes for imperial purposes, including the costs of maintaining convicts locally; a good many disliked convictism altogether; most disputed the imperial right to dictate land policy; and many, especially in South Australia, disapproved of the imperial government's directing that aid be given to religious denominations.

From the commencement of the era, the imperial government supported a freer market in land and labor across the colonies, not simply in South Australia. Thus, gifts of land halted in 1831 and were replaced by sales Attempts to construct a pastoral-lease system produced tremendous conflict, with colonists typically averse to any demand for payment.

In New South Wales in 1844, new rules even provoked thoughts of mutiny. Regarding employment, colonists agreed with the imperial encouragement of unrestricted migration, but controversy emerged over the convicts.

British opinion in the 1830s became more critical of the assignment of prisoners to private employers as redolent of slavery; it was abolished in 1840, and with it, transportation of convicts to the mainland largely halted, although growing numbers were transported to Tasmania.

The cessation of assignment eliminated the major virtue of transportation, from the colonists' standpoint, and hence led to a forceful agitation against its continuation. The British government ceased shipment to eastern Australia in 1852.

In Western Australia transportation began in 1850, at the colonists' desire, and continued until 1868. Altogether around 151,000 prisoners were transferred to eastern Australia and almost 10,000 to Western Australia.

In the early 1850s, the most spectacular political challenge stemmed from the gold rushes. Diggers (miners) hated tax imposition and the absence of properly representative institutions.

Discontent reached a crescendo at Ballarat, Victoria, where in December 1854, at the Eureka Stockade, troops and diggers battled, and some were murdered. The event is the most renowned of the few times in Australia's history involving violence among Europeans.

Common distrust of the imperial authority lessened, but did not eradicate, internal conflict among the colonists. Divisions of ideology and interest were fairly acute, especially in Sydney, where populist radicalism condemned persons of wealth, notably the major landholders.

The introduction of self-government signaled a leftward (but far from revolutionary) change in the internal power balance.

THE ECONOMY

The three decades preceding 1860 saw surges of the two bonanzas of Australian economic growth—wool and minerals.

Only then did persons, money, markets, and land availability intersect to prove that Australia was superbly adapted for cultivating fine wool. Occupation of Port Phillip was the most crucial component of a rush that pushed sheep raising 200 miles and beyond in an arc from beyond Adelaide in the south, north, and east to beyond Brisbane. The "squatter" pastoralist became an archetype of Australian history. Although it faced some slump in the early 1840s, the industry remained booming, and the whole eastern mainland profited as a consequence.

The first notable mineral discovery was that of copper in South Australia (1842 and 1845). The finding had the effect, to be repeated time and again, of unexpectedly rescuing an Australian region from stagnation.

Much more astonishing, however, was a reported sequence of gold discoveries made from 1851 onward, first in east-central New South Wales and subsequently across Victoria. As a result, Australia became a place of golden appeal.

The Victorian economy profited from the inflow of men and money, whereas the lesser colonies suffered. The Eureka Stockade incident notwithstanding, the diggers proved more boisterous than revolutionary.

AUSTRALIAN CULTURE AND CUSTOMS

Australian culture is a varied combination of Indigenous, European, and cosmopolitan influences. Australia's history of colonialism, immigration, and integration has molded the country's cultural environment, generating a unique combination of traditions, customs, and values.

Indigenous Australian culture is the oldest continuous culture in the world and has had a major effect on the creation of Australian identity. Indigenous Australians have a profound connection to the land and a rich spiritual and creative legacy, with art, storytelling, dance, and song playing a vital part in cultural expression.

European culture has also had a vital part in developing Australian culture, with British customs and ideals providing the foundation of many areas of Australian society. Sport, notably cricket and Australian Rules Football has long been a popular hobby, and the custom of the

"Aussie BBQ" has been a cornerstone of Australian social life.

Since the end of World War II, Australia has undergone tremendous immigration from nations all across the world, resulting in a lively and diversified multicultural culture. This has introduced new customs and traditions to Australia and has contributed to the country's unique cultural character.

One of the most noticeable elements of Australian culture is its informality and laid-back attitude, commonly referred to as the "Aussie way of life." Australians are usually sociable, and egalitarian, and have a strong feeling of mateship, or devotion to friends and comrades.

Australian English is a distinct dialect, with a distinctive vocabulary and accent that sets it different from other English-speaking nations. Slang and colloquialisms are ubiquitous in everyday speech, adding to the country's particular cultural character.

In terms of customs, Australians commemorate a multitude of national holidays, including Australia Day on January 26th and Anzac Day on April 25th. Christmas is also a popular holiday, celebrated in the heart of summer with customs such as beach barbecues and carol singalongs.

In summary, Australian culture is a unique combination of Indigenous, European, and multicultural elements, influenced by the country's history of colonialism, immigration, and integration. With a heavy focus on informality, mateship, and a love of the outdoors, Australian culture is noted for its laid-back and pleasant demeanor.

CHAPTER TWO

EXPLORING SYDNEY

Sydney is the largest and most lively city in Australia, famed for its magnificent beaches, iconic monuments, and rich cultural variety. Located on the east coast of Australia, Sydney is a flourishing metropolis that attracts millions of people every year from all over the world.

The city is named after Lord Sydney, the British Home Secretary who sanctioned the formation of the first European settlement in Australia in 1788. Since then, Sydney has developed to become a modern and global city, while yet keeping its historic beauty and character.

Sydney is famed for its spectacular natural features, such as the glittering seas of the harbor, the rocky cliffs of the coastline, and the lush greenery of its parks and gardens. Its cultural sector is also a key appeal, with a broad mix of museums, galleries, and performing arts venues displaying the finest of Australian and international talent.

The city is home to some of the world's most renowned structures, including the Sydney Opera House, the Sydney Harbour Bridge, and the Royal Botanic Garden, which are all must-see locations for tourists.

Sydney's lively and cosmopolitan population has also helped define the city's identity, with a diverse range of foods, festivals, and customs from throughout the world adding to its unique flavor.

Whether you're wanting to explore the great outdoors, experience the city's rich history and culture, or simply relax and soak up the sun on one of its gorgeous beaches, Sydney provides something for everyone.

Map of Sydney

ICONIC LANDMARKS IN SYDNEY

Sydney is home to some of the world's most recognizable monuments, which bring millions of visitors each year. From the architectural marvels of the Sydney Opera House and the Sydney Harbour Bridge to the natural beauty of the Royal Botanic Garden, seeing these icons is a must-do for every visitor to the city.

• THE SYDNEY OPERA HOUSE

The Sydney Opera House is one of the most recognizable monuments of Australia, located in the center of Sydney Harbor. This architectural wonder is a UNESCO World Heritage Site and one of the most frequented tourist spots in the country.

It is regarded to be one of the most recognized structures in the world and is noted for its unusual design, which makes it look like a sequence of white sail-like shells that appear to float on the lake.

The Sydney Opera House was conceived by Danish architect Jorn Utzon and the building began in 1959. It took 14 years to build and was officially inaugurated by Queen Elizabeth II in 1973.

The structure contains a succession of pre-cast concrete shells that are coated in over a million glazed white tiles, which reflect the sunlight and give the building its unique shimmering aspect.

The Opera House contains various performance rooms, including the Concert Hall, Opera Theatre, Drama Theatre, and Playhouse, which host a range of productions throughout the year.

The Concert Hall is the largest area and can accommodate up to 2,679 people. It is home to the Sydney Symphony Orchestra and showcases a mix of classical, contemporary, and popular music performances. The Opera Theatre is a more intimate facility and is typically utilized for opera and ballet events.

Visitors to the Opera House can take a guided tour of the structure, which gives a behind-the-scenes insight into the history and design of this renowned monument. The tour includes a visit to the main auditoriums, backstage spaces, and the Opera House's distinctive sail-like dome.

In addition to its performing venues, the Opera House is also home to various restaurants and bars, notably the Bennelong, which provides contemporary Australian cuisine and beautiful views of the harbor. Visitors may also take a stroll along the Opera House forecourt and enjoy the spectacular views of the harbor and city skyline.

The Sydney Opera House is a must-visit location for any tourist to Sydney. Its distinctive architecture, magnificent setting, and world-class performances make it one of f the most famous landmarks in the world. Whether you're interested in architecture, music, or just soaking in the atmosphere, the Sydney Opera House is an experience not to be missed.

The Sydney Opera House

• THE SYDNEY HARBOUR BRIDGE

The Sydney Harbour Bridge, commonly known as the "Coathanger," is another famous sight of Sydney, located in the center of Sydney Harbour. This engineering wonder is the biggest steel arch bridge in the world and is regarded to be one of the most iconic icons of Australia.

Construction of the Sydney Harbour Bridge began in 1923 and took eight years to complete. It was formally inaugurated in 1932 and has since become a major component of Sydney's skyline.

The bridge spans 1,149 meters (3,772 feet) and is supported by two large concrete pylons, which are 89 meters (292 feet) tall. The bridge contains eight lanes of traffic, as well as pedestrian and cycling pathways.

Visitors to Sydney may take a guided tour of the Sydney Harbour Bridge, which gives a unique viewpoint on this technical wonder. The trip includes a visit to the bridge's southeast pylon, which contains a museum and affords excellent views of the port and city skyline.

Visitors may also climb to the top of the bridge, which gives a stunning 360-degree panorama of the city and port. The climb is a wonderful experience and is ideal for individuals of all fitness levels.

In addition to its architectural marvel, the Sydney Harbour Bridge has become a significant aspect of Sydney's culture and history. It is the main point of Sydney's New Year's Eve celebrations when a spectacular fireworks show is conducted every year. The bridge has also been utilized in many movies and television series, reinforcing its place in popular culture.

The Sydney Harbour Bridge is also an important transit center, linking the city's north and south sides. It is utilized by approximately 200,000 automobiles and pedestrians every day and plays a significant part in the city's infrastructure.

Sydney Harbour Bridge

- **THE ROYAL BOTANICAL GARDEN**

The Royal Botanic rk in Sydney is a lovely
public park located in the center of the city, near
the Sydney Opera House and the Sydney
Harbour Bridge. Established in 1816, it is the
oldest scientific institution in Australia and has
become an essential component of Sydney's
cultural history.

The garden is stretched over 30 hectares (74 acres) of land and is home to an outstanding variety of native and exotic plants, including many rare and endangered species.

It provides tourists with a tranquil sanctuary amidst the hustle and bustle of the city, with lots of green areas, walking routes, and stunning panoramas to enjoy.

The Royal Botanic Garden is separated into numerous themed parts, each giving a distinct experience to visitors. The Palm Grove includes a variety of palms from throughout the world, while the Oriental Garden highlights the beauty of Asian flora.

The Herb Garden exhibits a diversity of herbs used for cooking and medicinal uses, while the Australian Rainforest Walk gives a view into the lush greenery and animals of the country's tropical areas.

The garden also boasts numerous special gardens, such as the Rose Garden, which features over 1,800 species of roses, and the Succulent Garden, which shows an outstanding variety of succulent plants from throughout the world.

Visitors may also have a picnic on the grounds or join a guided walk of the garden, which gives an insight into the history and significance of the plants and their ecosystems.

The Royal Botanic Garden is not just a destination of natural beauty but also an important research and conservation center. It houses various research institutions and laboratories that concentrate on the protection and preservation of endangered species and habitats.

The garden also conducts numerous educational programs and events, including seminars, lectures, and cultural festivals, allowing visitors to learn more about the plant world and its relevance.

Other notable landmarks in Sydney include the Sydney Tower Eye, which offers 360-degree views of the city from its observation deck, the Taronga Zoo, which is home to over 4,000 animals from around the world, and the Art Gallery of New South Wales, which features a diverse collection of Australian and international art.

In short, exploring the renowned sites of Sydney is a must-do for any tourist in the city. From the breathtaking architecture of the Sydney Opera House and Sydney Harbour Bridge to the natural beauty of the Royal Botanic Garden, these icons provide tourists an insight into the history and culture of this dynamic and varied city.

Royal Botanical Garden

Manly Beach is another popular site, located just a short boat trip from Sydney's core business center. The beach is recognized for its tranquil seas, making it great for swimming, kayaking, and stand-up paddleboarding. Visitors may take a stroll along the beachside promenade, have lunch at one of the numerous restaurants and cafés, or climb the adjacent North Head, which gives beautiful views of the harbor and city skyline.

- **THE SYDNEY TOWER EYE**

The Sydney Tower Eye is a prominent landmark located at the entrance of Sydney, Australia. Standing at a height of 309 meters (1,014 ft), it is the highest building in the city and one of the tallest structures in the Southern Hemisphere.

The tower was formerly called the Centrepoint Tower and was opened in 1981. It was created by the Australian architect Donald Crone and is built of reinforced concrete and steel. The tower received a substantial restoration in 2011, which included the installation of a new observation deck, a 4D theater, and a skywalk attraction.

The observation deck, located on the tower's top floors, offers amazing views over the city and its surrounding environs. Visitors may enjoy a 360-degree panoramic view of Sydney's prominent sites, such as the Sydney Opera House, the Sydney Harbour Bridge, and the Blue Mountains in the distance. The observation deck also has interactive touchscreens that give information about the city's history, culture, and geography.

The 4D cinema experience takes viewers on an exciting virtual voyage across Sydney, emphasizing its prominent sights and attractions. The cinema boasts state-of-the-art technology, including 3D images, surround sound, and special effects such as wind, rain, and even scents.

For the more brave, the skywalk attraction provides a unique experience, where visitors may walk on a glass platform that stretches out from the tower's edge, offering them a bird's eye view of the city below. The platform is placed 268 meters (880 feet) above the earth and offers an exciting and unique experience.

In addition to its observation deck and attractions, the Sydney Tower Eye is also home to various restaurants and cafés, including a rotating restaurant, which gives amazing views of the city as you dine.

The Sydney Tower Eye is not just a famous tourist attraction but also an essential element of Sydney's skyline and cultural legacy. It has become an icon of the city and a monument to its architectural brilliance and inventive spirit.

Sydney Tower Eye

BEACHES AND COASTAL AREAS

Sydney is blessed with some of the most beautiful beaches and coastal areas in the world, and it is no surprise that they are a major drawcard for visitors. The city has a wide range of beaches, from bustling surf spots to secluded coves, and each has its unique charm.

- ## BONDI BEACH

Bondi Beach is one of the most famous beaches in Australia and is located in the eastern suburbs of Sydney. It is a popular location for both locals and visitors, and is recognized for its stunning golden beaches, clear blue seas, and energetic environment.

Bondi Beach is a wonderful area for surfing, swimming, and sunbathing. The beach is roughly 1 kilometer (0.6 miles) long and is guarded by skilled lifeguards, making it a safe and entertaining destination for tourists of all ages.

The beach is also flanked by a choice of cafés, bars, and restaurants that serve up wonderful food and drinks. Visitors may get a bite to eat while enjoying spectacular views of the beach and water.

For those who are searching for something a bit more athletic, there are lots of things to enjoy at Bondi Beach. Visitors may take surfing lessons or rent surfboards and enjoy the waves. The beach also offers a skate park, beach volleyball courts, and a coastal walk that leads you around the lovely coastline.

Bondi Beach also organizes a variety of events throughout the year, including the iconic Bondi Open Air Cinema, where tourists may watch movies beneath the stars.

Despite its popularity, Bondi Beach manages to keep its particular charm and laid-back ambiance. It is a melting pot of ethnicities and countries, making it a perfect area to meet new people and take up the eclectic Sydney spirit.

In conclusion, Bondi Beach is a must-visit site for anybody visiting Sydney. It offers the perfect blend of sun, sand, and surf, as well as a dynamic environment and a selection of activities to enjoy. Whether you are wanting to relax on the beach, enjoy the surf, or explore the neighboring cafés and restaurants, Bondi Beach has something for everyone.

- **MANLY BEACH**

Manly Beach is another renowned beach located in the northern suburbs of Sydney, just a short boat trip away from Circular Quay. The beach is roughly 1.5 kilometers (0.9 miles) long and is recognized for its exceptional surf, crystal blue seas, and lovely natural environment.

The beach is separated into three areas: South Steyne, North Steyne, and Queenscliff. South Steyne is the major portion of the beach and is where you will find most of the services, including cafés, restaurants, and stores.

North Steyne is the calmer area of the beach and is a perfect place for families and people searching for a more serene ambiance. Queenscliff is the northernmost area of the beach and is popular with surfers.

Manly Beach is an excellent spot to swim, surf, and sunbathe. The beach is monitored by skilled lifeguards, making it a safe area for tourists of all ages. There are also lots of amenities, including showers, toilets, and changing rooms.

In addition to the beach itself, Manly also provides several attractions and activities to enjoy. The Corso is a famous pedestrian strip that stretches from the ferry station to the beach and is dotted with stores, cafés, and restaurants. Visitors may also take a trip along the Manly

Scenic Walkway, which offers spectacular views of the bay and coastline.

For individuals who are interested in learning more about the history of the area, there are a variety of museums and cultural sites in Manly. The Manly Art Gallery and Museum, for example, highlight the work of local artists and give insights into the history and culture of the area.

Manly Beach is also a wonderful site for water sports. Visitors may take surfing lessons, hire paddle boards or kayaks, or go on a whale-watching cruise. The beach is also host to a multitude of events and festivals throughout the year, including the Manly Jazz Festival and the Manly Food and Wine Festival.

Manly Beach is a terrific place for anybody visiting Sydney. It provides a magnificent natural backdrop, fantastic surf, and a selection of sights and activities to enjoy.

- PALM BEACH

Palm Beach is a picturesque beach located on the northernmost part of the Sydney coastline, about 41 kilometers (25 miles) from the city center. Known for its gorgeous natural landscape, crystal blue oceans, and golden sand, Palm Beach is a favorite destination for both locals and visitors alike.

One of the most prominent aspects of Palm Beach is its distinctive lighthouse, which rises at the northern extremity of the beach. The Barrenjoey Lighthouse is nearly 150 years old and gives magnificent views of the coastline and neighboring areas.

Visitors may take a guided tour of the lighthouse, which includes a climb to the top for stunning views of the ocean and surrounding scenery.

Palm Beach is also a popular area for swimming and surfing, with waves that are suited for all ability levels. The beach is monitored by skilled lifeguards, making it a safe area for tourists of all ages. In addition to swimming and surfing, guests may also take a stroll along the beach, sunbathe on the sand, or simply relax and take in the wonderful natural surroundings.

For those who are interested in exploring the surrounding region, Palm Beach has lots of attractions and activities to enjoy. The Ku-ring-gai Chase National Park is just a short drive away and provides a selection of hiking and walking routes, as well as spectacular views of the coastline and surrounding districts.

Palm Beach is also home to several restaurants and cafés, offering anything from casual seaside eating to upscale dining experiences. Visitors may enjoy fresh seafood, local wines, and a selection of foreign culinary alternatives.

Palm Beach is a lovely and serene resort that provides a selection of sights and activities for guests to enjoy. Whether you are wanting to relax on the beach, explore the surrounding region, or enjoy some wonderful cuisine, Palm Beach has something for everyone. With its spectacular natural beauty and laid-back ambiance, it's no wonder that Palm Beach is rated one of Sydney's greatest beaches.

- **WATSON BAY**

Watsons Bay is a lovely neighborhood located on the southern tip of Sydney Harbour, just a short boat ride from the city center. It is noted for its spectacular natural beauty, rich history, and relaxing seaside feel.

One of the most popular attractions in Watsons Bay is Gap Park, which affords beautiful views of the ocean and the rough coastline. Visitors may take a walk along the coastal route that snakes its way through the park, or simply relax on one of the numerous seats and take in the spectacular views.

Watsons Bay is also home to a selection of scenic beaches, including Camp Cove and Lady Bay Beach. Both of these beaches are great for swimming and sunbathing, with crystal-clear seas and smooth sand. Camp Cove also offers a small kiosk and a restaurant, where tourists may grab a bite to eat or a refreshing drink.

Another must-see site in Watsons Bay is the Hornby Lighthouse, which lies at the entrance to Sydney Harbour. The lighthouse is nearly 150 years old and affords spectacular views of the surrounding surroundings. Visitors may take a guided tour of the lighthouse, which includes a climb to the top for stunning views of the ocean and the surrounding environment.

For those who are interested in exploring the surrounding region, Watsons Bay has lots of attractions and activities to enjoy. The Sydney Harbour National Park is just a short distance away and provides a selection of hiking and walking routes, as well as spectacular views of the harbor and adjacent locations. Visitors may also take a boat journey to the adjacent Taronga Zoo, which is home to a diverse diversity of Australian species.

Watsons Bay is also home to several restaurants and cafés, offering anything from casual seaside eating to sophisticated dining experiences. Visitors may enjoy fresh seafood, local wines, and a selection of foreign culinary alternatives.

SYDNEY NEIGHBORHOODS

Sydney is a vibrant and cosmopolitan city that is made up of a diverse range of neighborhoods, each with its unique character and charm. From the bustling CBD to the trendy suburbs, there is something for everyone to discover and explore in this dynamic city.

One of the best ways to experience the true essence of Sydney is by venturing out into its diverse neighborhoods. Each neighborhood has its distinct personality and offers a different perspective on life in this bustling metropolis.

Whether you are interested in exploring the trendy cafes and boutique shops of Surry Hills, experiencing the bustling nightlife of Kings Cross, or soaking up the sun at the iconic Bondi Beach, Sydney's neighborhoods offer a wide range of attractions and activities to suit every taste and interest.

In this guide, we will take a closer look at some of Sydney's most popular neighborhoods, highlighting their unique features and must-see attractions. From the historical streets of The Rocks to the trendy bars and restaurants of Darlinghurst, we will explore the diverse neighborhoods that make Sydney such a fascinating and dynamic city. So pack your bags and get ready to discover the many faces of Sydney!

- **THE ROCKS**

The Rocks is one of Sydney's most recognizable suburbs, and is noted for its rich history and endearing character. Located just a stone's throw away from the Sydney Harbour Bridge and the Opera House, this area is one of the oldest in the city, with a history reaching back to the early 1800s.

The region was previously a rough and tumble neighborhood, home to sailors, prisoners, and other working-class people. Over time, though, the area began to gentrify, and many of the ancient buildings were maintained and repaired. Today, The Rocks is a popular location for visitors and residents alike, having a wide choice of sights and activities to discover.

One of the most prominent elements of The Rocks is its stunning historic architecture. The region is home to some of the oldest buildings in Sydney, with many of the structures going back to the early 19th century. Visitors may join a walking tour of the neighborhood to visit these ancient structures and learn about their unique history.

The Rocks is also recognized for its bustling environment and rich cultural scene. The district is home to a variety of galleries, museums, and cultural organizations, including the Museum of Contemporary Art and the Susannah Place Museum. It is also a famous place for live music and street performances, with a number of pubs and taverns hosting live music throughout the week.

Perhaps the most recognized attraction in The Rocks is the Saturday market. Every Saturday and Sunday, the streets of The Rocks come alive with a busy market, providing a wide choice of local crafts, cuisine, and souvenirs. Visitors may browse among the stalls, examining the items and enjoying local foods.

The Rocks is a fascinating area with a rich history and a unique character. Whether you are interested in discovering its ancient buildings, enjoying its active cultural scene, or simply soaking up its lovely ambiance, The Rocks is a must-visit location for anybody visiting Sydney.

• DARLINGHURST

Darlinghurst is a stylish suburb located in the heart of Sydney, just a stone's throw away from the central business area. Known for its bustling ambiance and colorful flair, Darlinghurst has long been a favorite destination for visitors and locals alike.

One of the most distinctive elements of Darlinghurst is its bustling nightlife. The neighborhood is home to a broad assortment of pubs, nightclubs, and live music venues, making it a popular destination for anyone wishing to experience Sydney's famed party scene.

From cozy cocktail bars to rowdy dance clubs, there is something for everyone in Darlinghurst's bustling nightlife scene.

In addition to its vibrant nightlife, Darlinghurst is also noted for its diversified cuisine scene. The neighborhood is home to a diverse assortment of restaurants, cafés, and diners, serving anything from gourmet cuisine to street food.

Beyond its nightlife and gastronomic offers, Darlinghurst is also home to a bustling arts and culture scene. The district is home to a multitude of galleries, theaters, and performance places, presenting the finest of Sydney's creative talent.

Visitors may enjoy a play at the famed Hayes Theatre, peruse contemporary art at the Maunsell Wickes Gallery, or take in a film at the Palace Verona cinema.

Darlinghurst is also a popular location for shopping, with a wide choice of shops and specialized businesses selling anything from antique apparel to designer items. Visitors may explore the beautiful side lanes and laneways of the area, uncovering hidden jewels and unusual finds along the way.

- **SURRY HILLS**

Surry Hills is a bustling and colorful area located in the eastern suburbs of Sydney. Known for its varied population, fashionable eateries, and booming cultural scene, Surry Hills has become one of the city's most popular attractions in recent years.

One of the biggest charms of Surry Hills is the . The neighborhood is home to a diverse assortment of cafés, restaurants, and pubs, serving anything from gourmet cuisine to informal street food.

From brunch cafes and bakeries to fine dining restaurants and cocktail bars, Surry Hills offers something to suit every taste and budget.

In addition to its numerous gastronomic choices, Surry Hills is also home to a variety of stylish shops and speciality retailers. Visitors may explore the neighborhood's beautiful side alleys and laneways, uncovering hidden jewels and unusual finds along the way.

Beyond its gastronomic and retail options, Surry Hills is also noted for its strong arts and cultural scene. The area is home to a multitude of galleries, performance spaces, and live music venues, presenting the finest of Sydney's creative talent.

Visitors may enjoy a show at the renowned Belvoir St Theatre, peruse contemporary art at the White Rabbit Gallery, or take in a live music performance at the Golden Age Cinema & Bar.

Surry Hills is also home to a variety of historic sites and cultural organizations, including the Sydney Jewish Museum and the Surry Hills Library. Visitors may explore the neighborhood's rich history and cultural heritage, learning about the area's early settlers and significant personalities.

- **PADDINGTON**

Paddington is a lovely and historic neighborhood located in the eastern suburbs of Sydney. Known for its Victorian terrace houses, tree-lined avenues, and lively commercial environment, Paddington is a favorite destination for both locals and tourists.

One of the biggest charms of Paddington is its boutique retail sector. The neighborhood is home to a diverse selection of specialty retailers, small boutiques, and brand fashion labels, offering anything from antique apparel to high-end designer attire. Visitors may browse the stores on Oxford Street, discover the boutiques on William Street, or investigate the Paddington Markets for unique handcrafted crafts and souvenirs.

Beyond its commercial offers, Paddington is also home to a variety of cultural organizations and historic buildings. The neighborhood is home to the Victoria Barracks, a historic military district that goes back to the mid-1800s, and the Paddington Reservoir Gardens, a beautifully restored public park that highlights the area's rich history and architecture.

Paddington is also noted for its robust arts and cultural scene. The area is home to a multitude of galleries, performance spaces, and live music venues, presenting the finest of Sydney's creative talent. Visitors may attend a show at the Seymour Centre, peruse contemporary art at the Maunsell Wickes Gallery, or take in a live music performance at the Paddington RSL Club.

In addition to its cultural activities, Paddington is also home to a multitude of restaurants, cafés, and pubs. Visitors may experience food from around the world, have a coffee in one of the neighborhood's numerous cafés, or relax with a drink at a local bar.

Paddington is a bustling and varied area with a lot to offer tourists. Whether you are interested in shopping, culture, or history, Paddington is a must-visit place for anybody wishing to enjoy the finest of Sydney.

• BONDI

Bondi is a world-famous coastal town located in the eastern suburbs of Sydney, noted for its gorgeous beach, bustling environment, and laid-back lifestyle. Bondi Beach is a crescent-shaped length of beach that attracts locals and visitors alike, lured to its crystal-clear seas and stunning views. The beach is monitored by lifeguards and provides a range of activities, including surfing, swimming, and sunbathing.

Beyond the beach, Bondi is home to a varied variety of inhabitants, with a mix of travellers, students, and young professionals calling the region home.

The area offers a dynamic environment, with a thriving eating and entertainment scene that appeals to all tastes and budgets. Visitors may find everything from fancy restaurants to informal cafés, along with a choice of pubs and nightclubs.

Bondi is also noted for its vibrant arts and cultural scene. The area is home to a multitude of galleries, theaters, and music venues, presenting the finest of Sydney's creative talent.

Visitors may enjoy a play at the Bondi Pavilion Theatre, peruse modern art at the Bondi Art Lounge, or take in a live music performance at the Beach Road Hotel.

One of the most famous attractions in Bondi is the Bondi to Coogee Coastal Walk, a gorgeous walking track that makes its way down the coast and gives spectacular views of the ocean and surrounding surroundings.

The walk is around six kilometers long and runs past a number of parks, beaches, and cliffs, allowing lots of opportunity to take in the natural beauty of the area.

For those interested in health and wellbeing, Bondi is also home to a variety of yoga studios, fitness facilities, and wellness retreats. The neighborhood has a strong focus on healthy living, with many inhabitants taking part in outdoor activities and fitness programs.

FOOD AND DRINKS

Sydney is a multicultural city that provides a varied selection of meals and drinks. Whether you're in the mood for traditional Australian cuisine or unusual cuisines from across the world, you'll find plenty of alternatives in Sydney.

One of the most iconic foods in Sydney is the pork pie. This pastry stuffed with delicious minced beef and sauce is a typical Australian delicacy that can be found in bakeries and cafés around the city. Another iconic Australian food is fish and chips, which is best served with a side of tartar sauce and a cool beer.

Sydney also boasts a flourishing cafe culture, with several fashionable coffee shops and brunch locations.

The city's passion of coffee is mirrored in its high-quality brews, with many cafés employing locally roasted beans and providing a range of brewing methods, from pour-overs to cold brews.

For those searching for exotic delicacies, Sydney's multiculturalism means that you may enjoy real food from all over the world. Some popular international meals include Vietnamese pho, Japanese sushi, Italian pizza and pasta, and Indian curries.

In recent years, Sydney has also been recognized for its craft beer culture, with several local breweries cropping up across the city. These brewers provide a range of unusual and tasty beers, from hoppy IPAs to velvety stouts.

Wine aficionados will also appreciate Sydney's closeness to the Hunter Valley wine area, which produces some of Australia's greatest wines.

In terms of nightlife, Sydney boasts a number of alternatives for those wishing to unwind with a drink or dance the night away. The city's fashionable pubs and nightclubs offer everything from artisan drinks to live music and DJ performances.

Sydney's food and drink industry is diversified, lively, and continually developing. Whether you're seeking for typical Australian meals, foreign flavors, or artisan cocktails, you're sure to find something that meets your interests in this dynamic city.

Pork Pie

CULTURAL ACTIVITIES

Sydney is a city that is rich in culture and provides a choice of experiences for those who are interested in learning about its history, art, and customs.

One of the most famous cultural experiences in Sydney is visiting the Sydney Opera House, a UNESCO World Heritage Site that is acknowledged as one of the most significant buildings of the 20th century.

The Opera House is not only a monument for its remarkable architecture, but also a hub for performing arts, featuring a range of events and concerts throughout the year.

For individuals interested in Aboriginal culture, Sydney provides a choice of activities that exhibit the history and customs of Australia's Indigenous peoples. The Museum of Contemporary Art Australia and the Art Gallery of New South Wales both feature collections of contemporary Aboriginal art, while the Royal Botanic Garden Sydney offers guided tours that focus on the traditional usage of plants by Aboriginal people.

Sydney also boasts a lively street art movement, with murals and installations across the city that promote local and international artists. The Newtown area is particularly recognized for its street art, with many buildings and walls covered with colorful and thought-provoking sculptures.

For a more full cultural experience, travelers may attend festivals and events that highlight Sydney's varied populations. The Sydney Lunar Festival, for example, is an annual celebration of Chinese New Year that includes dragon boat racing, lantern displays, and cultural performances. The annual Vivid Sydney festival is also a famous event that mixes light displays, music, and speeches, converting the city into a beautiful outdoor gallery.

OUTDOOR ACTIVITIES

Sydney is a city that enjoys a gorgeous natural setting, making it the perfect location for outdoor enthusiasts. The city and its neighboring surroundings provide a multitude of activities that appeal to diverse interests and ability levels.

One of the most popular outdoor activities in Sydney is hiking. The city is surrounded by national parks, and there are a number of paths that give spectacular views of the port, coastline, and hinterland.

Some of the most popular hiking pathways are the Bondi to Coogee coastal walk, the Spit Bridge to Manly trail, and the Royal National Park coastal track.

Sydney is also famed for its gorgeous beaches, and there are a multitude of water-based activities accessible for visitors. Surfing is a popular hobby, and there are surf schools located at several of the beaches around the city.

Kayaking and stand-up paddleboarding are additional popular pastimes, with guided trips available that explore the harbor and coastline.

For those who prefer to stay on land, Sydney provides a selection of bike routes that showcase the city's natural beauty. The Sydney Harbour Bridge is a popular riding location, with a designated bike lane affording beautiful views of the bay. Other popular riding routes include the Centennial Park cycleway and the Bay Run.

In addition to these activities, Sydney also provides a selection of adventure sports such as rock climbing, abseiling, and bungee jumping. There are also outdoor exercise sessions offered in many of the parks throughout the city, allowing an opportunity to be active while enjoying the gorgeous surroundings.

SHOPPING AND DINING

Sydney is a city that provides a broad selection of shopping and dining experiences, from luxury shops and high-end restaurants to eccentric markets and street food sellers. Here are some of the top locations to shop and dine in Sydney:

The Rocks: The Rocks is recognized for its artisanal stores and boutiques, selling unique and handmade items. There are also a choice of restaurants and cafés dishing up wonderful food from across the world.

Queen Victoria Building: The Queen Victoria Building is a stunning heritage building that provides a selection of high-end boutiques and designer retailers. The building itself is a piece of art, with gorgeous architecture and complex features. There are also a number of cafés and restaurants offering anything from exquisite dining to casual eats.

Pitt Street Mall: Pitt Street Mall is one of Sydney's best shopping locations, featuring a mix of local and international brands. The pedestrianized boulevard is studded with stores, cafés, and restaurants, making it a perfect area to spend a day shopping and dining.

Paddington Markets: Located in the fashionable Paddington district, the Paddington Markets provide a choice of handcrafted items and unusual gifts. The markets are open on Saturdays and provide a mix of fashion, art, and crafts.

Sydney Fish Market: Sydney Fish Market is the largest fish market in the Southern Hemisphere, offering a selection of fresh seafood and fish. Visitors may browse the market, sample the seafood, and even attend a culinary lesson to learn how to make it themselves.

Chinatown: Sydney's Chinatown is a vibrant and bustling neighbourhood, featuring a selection of Chinese restaurants and businesses. Visitors may enjoy traditional Chinese food, purchase for souvenirs, and explore the colorful streets and alleyways of this vibrant area.

Sydney provides a varied selection of shopping and dining experiences, from upscale shops to eccentric markets and street food sellers. Whether you're seeking for high-end clothes, artisanal items, or excellent cuisine, you'll find it all in this busy city.

SYDNEY NIGHTLIFE

Sydney's nightlife is bustling and varied, offering something for everyone. Whether you're searching for a quiet drink in a snug pub or a night out on the town dancing the night away, Sydney offers it all.

One of the most famous nightlife venues in Sydney is Kings Cross, which has a reputation for being the city's party area. Here, you'll discover a mix of pubs and nightclubs, including some of the city's most renowned locations.

From the iconic Oxford Art Factory to the small, speakeasy-style Eau de Vie, Kings Cross has lots to offer for those seeking for a vibrant night out.

Another famous neighbourhood for nightlife in Sydney is Darlinghurst, which is home to some of the city's trendiest pubs and restaurants. This suburb has a laid-back, bohemian air and is popular with a younger audience.

Some of the top bars in Darlinghurst are Shady Pines Saloon, a dive bar with a western motif, and The Cliff Dive, which offers up tiki drinks in a bright, tropical environment.

If you're searching for a more upmarket evening experience, go to the Sydney CBD. Here, you'll discover a choice of high-end pubs and nightclubs, including the spectacular Ivy nightclub and rooftop bar, and the luxury Establishment Hotel.

For those who want a more calm nighttime experience, Sydney has lots of alternatives too.

From rooftop bars with breathtaking views of the city skyline to small wine bars nestled away in the city's laneways, there are plenty of places to unwind with a drink after a long day of sightseeing.

Sydney's nightlife culture is broad and vibrant, with lots of alternatives for every taste and budget. Whether you're searching for a crazy night out or a quiet drink with pals, you're sure to find it in this dynamic city.

CHAPTER THREE

MELBOURNE AND VICTORIA

Melbourne is the capital city of Victoria, one of Australia's most varied and attractive states. Known for its thriving arts and cultural scene, gorgeous landscapes, and world-class cuisine, Melbourne and Victoria give tourists a unique and remarkable experience.

Melbourne is a cosmopolitan city that offers a rich past and a flourishing modern culture. From the classic Flinders Street Station to the fashionable laneways dotted with street art and coffee shops, Melbourne is a city that is both attractive and intriguing.

It is also recognized for its love of sport, with the Melbourne Cricket Ground and Rod Laver Arena hosting some of the world's major sports events.

Victoria is a state that is blessed with natural beauty, with magnificent coastline, rolling hills, and lush woods. From the Great Ocean Road to the Yarra Valley wine area, Victoria is a wonderland for people who enjoy the great outdoors. The state is also home to some of Australia's most unusual species, including kangaroos, koalas, and echidnas.

Melbourne and Victoria are also famed for their world-class food and drink culture. From the iconic coffee shops of Melbourne to the vineyards of the Yarra Valley, there is no shortage of wonderful food and drink to be enjoyed in this state.

TOP ATTRACTIONS IN MELBOURNE

Here are some of the attractions in Melbourne;

• THE FEDERATION SQUARE

Federation Square is a unique public place located in the center of Melbourne, Australia. It was inaugurated in 2002 to mark the centennial of the Federation of Australia and has since become a popular attraction for residents and visitors alike.

One of the most prominent elements of Federation Square is its architecture. The square comprises a collection of interconnected buildings and outdoor areas that were created to showcase Melbourne's contemporary and varied culture.

The structures are composed of sandstone, zinc, and glass, and are meant to be ecologically sustainable. The design has won several prizes for architecture and has been commended for its creativity and urban integration.

Federation Square is also a center of cultural activities in Melbourne. The area holds a multitude of events and activities throughout the year, including music performances, art exhibitions, and cultural festivals.

The square is home to the Australian Centre for the Moving Image (ACMI), which highlights Australian and worldwide cinema, television, and digital culture. Visitors may also tour the Ian Potter Centre: NGV Australia, which contains the National Gallery of Victoria's Australian art collection.

In addition to its cultural attractions, Federation Square is also home to a number of restaurants, cafés, and pubs. Visitors may have a meal or a drink while taking in views of the area and the surrounding city.

The Federation Square

- **THE MELBOURNE CRICKET GROUND**

The Melbourne Cricket Ground (MCG), popularly known as "The G," is a renowned sports venue located in Yarra Park, Melbourne, Australia. It is the largest stadium in the southern hemisphere and has a seating capacity of approximately 100,000 people.

The MCG is predominantly used for cricket and Australian rules football, but it has also held numerous other events, including concerts, religious groups, and political demonstrations. It is the home ground of the Melbourne Cricket Club and the Melbourne Football Club, two of Australia's oldest and most prominent sporting organizations.

The MCG has a rich history that extends back to the 1850s when the first cricket matches were played on the venue. The initial grandstand was completed in 1854, and the stadium has since undergone several restorations and extensions to become the world-class venue it is today.

One of the most remarkable elements of the MCG is its unusual oval shape, which provides for unimpeded views from all seats. The stadium also includes a retractable roof that may be closed in case of adverse weather.

In addition to its sporting facilities, the MCG is also home to the National sporting Museum, which displays the history and achievements of Australian sport. The museum contains interactive exhibitions, unique artifacts, and memorabilia from some of Australia's most prominent sportsmen and teams.

The MCG is not merely a sports arena but an iconic symbol of Melbourne. Its rich history, state-of-the-art facilities, and cultural relevance make it a must-visit site for sports lovers and visitors alike.

- **NATIONAL GALLERY OF VICTORIA**

The National Gallery of Victoria (NGV) is the oldest and most visited art museum in Australia. Located in Melbourne, Victoria, it holds a significant collection of Australian, European, Asian, and modern art, including paintings, sculptures, ceramics, and decorative arts.

The NGV was formed in 1861 and has since evolved to become one of the most prominent cultural institutions in the country. It is separated into two campuses, the NGV International and the Ian Potter Centre: NGV Australia, both located in the city of Melbourne.

NGV International, located in the heart of Melbourne's arts area, houses the gallery's international collection. It exhibits about 70,000 items, including a large collection of European art, ranging from the Renaissance era to modern works. Some of the highlights of the collection include pieces by Rembrandt, Rubens, and Picasso.

The Ian Potter Centre: NGV Australia, located in Federation Square, shows the gallery's Australian art collection. It displays works from Australian Indigenous artists, as well as Australian art from the colonial period to modern works. The center also contains a range of exhibitions and events geared to engage visitors with Australian art.

The NGV also offers a number of temporary exhibits throughout the year, showcasing both national and international artists. These exhibitions encompass a range of subjects and genres, giving visitors a chance to explore a varied spectrum of art forms and techniques.

Apart from the exhibitions, the NGV also provides a range of programs and activities for visitors of all ages, including guided tours, seminars, workshops, and events. The gallery also features a shop and café on site, allowing visitors to take a break and soak up the ambiance.

The National Gallery of Victoria is a must-visit place for anybody interested in art and culture. Its world-class collection, wide range of exhibitions and events, and gorgeous building make it an important element of any visit to Melbourne.

National Gallery of Victoria

National Gallery of Victoria

- **QUEEN VICTORIA MARKET**

Queen Victoria Market is one of Melbourne's most famous tourist attractions, and it is also the biggest open-air market in the Southern Hemisphere.

Located on the crossroads of Elizabeth and Victoria Streets, the market is spread over seven hectares and contains a broad range of vendors providing fresh fruit, meats, seafood, deli products, baked goods, apparel, jewelry, souvenirs, and more.

The market has a long history dating back to the 1850s when it was a cattle market. In the late 1800s, it became a wholesale fruit and vegetable market, and in the 1900s, it turned into the retail market that we know today.

The market was formally dubbed the Queen Victoria Market in commemoration of Queen Victoria's Diamond Jubilee in 1897.

The market is a buzzing center of activity, with sellers offering everything from fresh fruits and vegetables to homemade crafts and souvenirs.

Visitors may wander through the market's several aisles and visit the stalls, enjoying fresh vegetables, cheeses, and other culinary pleasures. The market is also home to various cafes and food vendors, offering a range of wonderful cuisine.

In addition to the food and shopping, the Queen Victoria Market also holds other events throughout the year, including night markets, culinary festivals, and cultural festivities. These events give visitors the opportunity to experience the market's dynamic atmosphere and discover new and fascinating items.

- **MELBOURNE ZOO**

Melbourne Zoo, commonly known as the Royal Melbourne Zoological Gardens, is a major tourist site in Melbourne, Victoria, Australia. It was opened in 1862, making it Australia's oldest zoo, and is located just north of the city center in the neighborhood of Parkville.

The Melbourne Zoo is home to more than 320 animal species from Australia and throughout the world, including several endangered and unusual species. Visitors may observe creatures such as Asian elephants, lions, tigers, gorillas, orangutans, and koalas, among many more.

The zoo features numerous locations and displays that depict the animals in their natural habitats. Visitors may tour the Trail of the Elephants, where they can witness the zoo's family of Asian elephants, including the youngest member, Mali. The Gorilla jungle exhibit is a big, immersive jungle enclosure that allows guests to experience the gorillas in a genuine setting.

The zoo is also home to a huge Australian animal display, containing kangaroos, wallabies, emus, wombats, and other local species. Visitors may tour the Australian Bush exhibit to learn about the unusual flora and creatures found in Australia's dry areas.

In addition to its animal displays, Melbourne Zoo offers a range of educational programs and activities for visitors of all ages. There are guided tours, animal interactions, and opportunities to learn about conservation initiatives and the necessity of maintaining species and their habitats.

Overall, Melbourne Zoo is a must-visit sight for animal enthusiasts and anybody wishing to experience the beauty and diversity of Australia's biodiversity. With its world-class exhibitions, educational activities, and commitment to conservation, it is a vital cultural institution in Victoria and a cherished destination for tourists from across the world.

• EUREKA TOWER

The Eureka Tower is a 297.3-meter (975-foot) skyscraper located in the Southbank neighborhood of Melbourne, Victoria. It was built in 2006 and was named after the Eureka Stockade, an uprising that took place in 1854 in Ballarat, Victoria.

The Eureka Tower is the highest skyscraper in Melbourne and the second-tallest building in Australia, behind the Q1 tower on the Gold Coast. It is also one of the highest residential structures in the world, with 556 units spread over 91 levels.

The tower's observation deck, dubbed the Eureka Skydeck, is positioned on the 88th level and offers amazing panoramic views of the city and its surrounds. The deck is 285 meters (935 feet) high and has a glass cube nicknamed "The Edge," which stretches out from the building's edge, providing guests an exciting view of the city below.

The Eureka Tower also includes a number of additional services, including offices, restaurants, and a hotel. The tower's design was inspired by the form of a golden ratio, and its unique gold-colored facade is made up of thousands of individual glass panels.

Visitors to the Eureka Tower may take a high-speed elevator to the 88th story, where they can enjoy amazing views of Melbourne and beyond. The Eureka Skydeck also contains a selection of interactive displays and exhibitions that illustrate the tower's history, architecture, and engineering.

- **KILDA BEACH**

St. Kilda Beach is one of the most popular beaches in Melbourne, located just six kilometers from the city center. The beach is bordered by a vibrant coastal area with plenty of attractions and things to do.

The beach provides a lengthy stretch of white sand and crystal blue sea, great for swimming, sunbathing, and surfing. There are also lots of beach activities accessible, such as beach volleyball, kite surfing, and windsurfing. St. Kilda Beach also provides different services, including lifeguards, showers, changing rooms, and grilling facilities.

One of the most prominent sights near St. Kilda Beach is the St. Kilda Pier, which is a popular place for fishing and gives spectacular views of the Melbourne cityscape. The pier is also home to a colony of small penguins, and tourists may join a guided tour to observe them up close.

The St. Kilda Esplanade Market is another must-visit sight. The market is open every Sunday and includes a choice of arts & crafts, fashion, and food vendors, making it the perfect spot to pick up souvenirs or gifts.

There are also lots of restaurants, cafés, and pubs in the neighborhood, making it a fantastic site for a relaxing lunch or supper after a day at the beach. The historic Luna Park is also located nearby, featuring exhilarating rides and carnival activities for guests of all ages

- MELBOURNE MUSEUM

Melbourne Museum is one of the largest and most visited museums in Australia, located in Carlton Gardens. The museum contains a huge collection of natural and cultural history exhibits and is a fantastic site to discover the history, culture, and environment of Melbourne and Australia.

The museum offers a unique and dynamic approach of presenting knowledge that interests visitors of all ages.

The museum's natural history halls display a varied diversity of Australian animals and flora. Visitors may learn about Australia's ancient past and witness a diversity of fossils, including the world-famous big squid, enormous squid, and dinosaurs. The museum also contains a specific department for the study of insects, showing a collection of over 500,000 specimens.

The cultural history galleries are dedicated to the history and culture of the people of Melbourne and Victoria. The galleries represent diverse facets of human existence, including art, music, fashion, and technology.

The Bunjilaka Aboriginal Cultural Centre within the museum is a wonderful site to learn about the history and culture of the indigenous people of Victoria.

The museum also hosts various temporary exhibitions throughout the year, highlighting diverse themes and issues. These shows vary from art, science, and history, and are always thought-provoking and fascinating.

For youngsters, there is a special children's gallery named the Pauline Gandel Children's Gallery. It's a fantastic environment for youngsters to study and play at the same time. The gallery features interactive exhibitions, hands-on games, and engaging displays that interest children of all ages.

In addition to the exhibitions, the museum also offers a gift shop and cafe. The gift store includes a choice of souvenirs, books, and presents relating to the museum and Melbourne, while the café serves a variety of great cuisine and drinks.

- **YARRA RIVER CRUISE**

A Yarra River Cruise is one of the greatest ways to enjoy the beauty and charm of Melbourne, as it gives breathtaking views of the city's skyline, as well as the chance to learn about the city's history and culture. The Yarra River, which runs through the heart of Melbourne, is an iconic waterway that has played a key part in the development of the city from its establishment in 1835.

A typical Yarra River Cruise begins at Southbank, where guests board a luxurious boat that takes them on a picturesque cruise around the city. The boat glides along the river, passing past some of Melbourne's most famous monuments, including the Melbourne Cricket Ground, the Royal Botanic Gardens, and Federation Square.

The commentary supplied by the informed crew members gives depth and perspective to the views, providing passengers a deeper understanding for the history and value of the locations they are experiencing.

One of the joys of a Yarra River Cruise is the ability to observe Melbourne from a fresh perspective. As the boat glides along the river, guests may enjoy panoramic views of the city's cityscape, which is particularly magnificent at night when the skyscrapers are lighted up with bright lights. The river itself is also a sight to see, with its gentle currents and serene waters providing a quiet ambiance that is a dramatic contrast to the bustling city streets.

A Yarra River Cruise is also a terrific chance to learn about Melbourne's rich history and culture. The crew members give intelligent commentary during the tour, sharing intriguing information and stories about the towns and landmarks that are passed along the way.

This may be especially instructive for visitors who are visiting Melbourne for the first time, since it provides them a greater grasp of the city's past and present.

OUTDOOR ACTIVITIES IN VICTORIA

Victoria is a state in Australia that is known for its stunning natural beauty and offers a wide range of outdoor activities for adventure enthusiasts. Here are some of the top outdoor activities in Victoria you can explore:

- **HIKING**

Victoria is home to some of the most outstanding hiking routes in Australia, offering a range of experiences from easy walks to demanding excursions that will take you through rocky terrain and stunning vistas. Here are some of the top hiking paths in Victoria:

The Grampians National Park: Located in Western Victoria, The Grampians is a must-visit location for hiking aficionados. The park is home to a diverse variety of species and has a number of picturesque paths, including the difficult Grampians Peaks Trail, which takes you through some of the area's most spectacular landscape.

Wilsons Promontory National Park: Located near the southernmost edge of mainland Australia, Wilsons Promontory is a magnificent coastal park with a selection of hiking routes to explore. The Prom's most renowned trek is the 3-day Wilsons Promontory Circuit, which takes you along gorgeous coastline and into lush woodlands.

The Great Ocean Walk: One of Victoria's most popular hiking paths, the Great Ocean Walk spans for almost 100km along the magnificent coastline of the Great Ocean Road. The walk takes you past some of the region's most picturesque sights, including the Twelve Apostles and the Cape Otway Lighthouse.

The Alpine National Park: Located in the northeast of Victoria, the Alpine National Park is a stunning wilderness region that provides a selection of hiking paths for all levels of fitness.

The park is home to some of Victoria's highest peaks, including Mount Bogong and Mount Feathertop, and has a choice of paths that will take you through pristine alpine forests and through crystal clear mountain streams.

The Dandenong Ranges: Located just a short drive from Melbourne, the Dandenong Ranges are a popular destination for hikers and nature enthusiasts. The park is home to a multitude of picturesque routes, including the famed 1000 Steps Walk, which takes you up a steep hillside to breathtaking views of the surrounding area.

No matter what your skill level or hiking preferences, there is something for everyone in Victoria's broad collection of hiking routes. So grab your hiking boots, pack a picnic, and set out to experience some of the state's most spectacular natural surroundings.

- **SURFING**

Victoria is home to some of Australia's top surfing sites, with waves that appeal to both beginners and specialists. From the iconic Bells Beach to the more remote beaches along the Great Ocean Road, Victoria has plenty to offer for any surfing enthusiast.

Bells Beach is one of the most renowned surf places in Victoria, located around an hour and a half drive from Melbourne. The beach is noted for its huge swells that provide perfect conditions for expert surfers. It is also host to the Rip Curl Pro, one of the world's most prominent surfing contests.

Other renowned surfing places in Victoria include Torquay, which is noted for its long, mellow waves that are great for novices. Jan Juc is another famous destination, located just a few minutes away from Torquay. The beach features regular waves that are appropriate for surfers of all abilities.

Further along the Great Ocean Road, you'll find some of Victoria's most remote surf beaches. Winkipop, Johanna Beach, and Bells Beach are all well-known sites that deliver good waves, but you'll need to be prepared for a bit of a trek to get there.

If you're searching for a surf instruction, there are many of surf schools along the coast that cater to beginners. The schools provide equipment, including wetsuits and surfboards, and teachers to educate you through the basics of surfing.

Some schools also offer surf camps for people who wish to immerse themselves in the surf culture for a few days or weeks.

When it comes to surfing in Victoria, it's vital to be mindful of the weather conditions and any risks, such as rips and currents. It's usually a good idea to check the weather and surf forecasts before venturing out, and never surf alone. With adequate preparation and competence, Victoria's surf areas may deliver an outstanding surfing experience.

• SKIING AND SNOWBOARDING

Victoria is a popular location for skiing and snowboarding in Australia, with a selection of resorts and slopes appropriate for all levels of expertise.

The snow season normally extends from early June to early October, depending on the weather conditions. Here are some of the greatest spots for skiing and snowboarding in Victoria:

Mount Buller: Located three hours from Melbourne, Mount Buller is one of the most popular ski destinations in Victoria, with 22 lifts and over 80 slopes catering to all levels of ability.

Falls Creek: Situated in the Alpine National Park, Falls Creek has over 90 lines split across four separate terrain parks, making it a popular destination for both skiers and snowboarders.

Mount Hotham: With a peak elevation of 1,861 meters, Mount Hotham offers some of the finest views of the Victorian Alps. The resort boasts about 320 hectares of skiable terrain and is noted for its steep slopes.

Mount Baw Baw: Located in Gippsland, Mount Baw Baw is the nearest ski resort to Melbourne, making it a popular day-trip destination. The resort provides a mix of slopes appropriate for beginners and intermediate skiers and snowboarders.

Mount Buffalo: Situated in the Alpine National Park, Mount Buffalo provides a range of snow-based sports, including cross-country skiing, snowshoeing, and tobogganing. The resort is recognized for its spectacular views of the surrounding mountains and valleys.

In addition to skiing and snowboarding, there are many other winter sports accessible in Victoria, including snowmobiling, snowshoeing, and ice-skating. Many resorts also offer a selection of après-ski activities, such as hot tubs, saunas, and spas, giving the perfect way to unwind after a day on the slopes.

• ROCK CLIMBING

Rock climbing is a popular outdoor sport in Victoria, Australia, drawing both residents and visitors from across the world. The state provides a multitude of climbing options, from rocky coastline cliffs to the towering peaks of the Victorian Alps.

Rock climbing in Victoria may be an amazing and hard activity, requiring strength, endurance, and mental focus. The sport requires mounting high rock faces with specialized equipment, including harnesses, ropes, carabiners, and other safety gear.

Victoria's diverse terrain offers a selection of rock climbing experiences ideal for climbers of all abilities, from beginners to specialists. Popular climbing sites in Victoria include the Grampians National Park, Mount Arapiles, and the You Yangs.

The Grampians, in particular, are a world-renowned climbing destination, having more than 5,000 routes over a range of rock types and grades.

The region is home to some of Australia's most renowned and hard climbs, including Taipan Wall, regarded by many to be one of the top sport climbing locations in the world.

However, rock climbing in Victoria is not without its perils, and climbers must take necessary safety steps to preserve their well-being.

Climbers are urged to climb with experienced partners, utilize adequate safety equipment, and follow suggested climbing procedures, such as avoiding climbs during harsh weather conditions.

- **KAYAKING AND CANOEING**

Kayaking and canoeing are popular water-based recreational sports that entail paddling a small boat across water. Both hobbies share similarities in terms of equipment and procedures but differ in boat design, paddle type, and skill level required.

Kayaking includes paddling a kayak, which is a low-profile watercraft that is generally driven by a double-bladed paddle. Kayaks come in all forms and sizes, and they are built for diverse water situations, such as calm lakes, rivers, and whitewater rapids.

Kayaking is a versatile activity that may be done solo or in a group, and it can be enjoyed for pleasure or as a competitive sport.

Canoeing, on the other hand, requires paddling a canoe, which is an open-top watercraft that is powered by a single-bladed paddle. Canoes are often bigger and more stable than kayaks, and they are meant for slower-moving water, such as lakes and rivers. Canoeing is frequently considered as a more leisurely and sociable sport compared to kayaking, and it is popular for family trips and scenic tours.

Both kayaking and canoeing require a minimum degree of fitness and adequate paddling technique. Proper paddling technique entails using the core muscles to propel the paddle stroke, rather than depending exclusively on the arms. Paddlers also need to have strong balance and coordination to maintain stability and control of the boat.

Victoria, Australia, is home to a number of rivers that are excellent for kayaking and canoeing. The Yarra River, for example, passes through Melbourne and provides a lovely path for kayaking and canoeing trips.

The Gippsland Lakes, located in eastern Victoria, are a network of lakes and waterways that offer possibilities for both kayaking and canoeing. The Murray River, which forms part of the boundary between Victoria and New South Wales, is another popular site for paddling enthusiasts.

When indulging in kayaking and canoeing in Victoria, it is necessary to observe safety norms and laws. Paddlers should always wear a personal flotation device (PFD) and carry required safety equipment, such as a whistle and a signaling device.

Paddlers should also be careful of weather conditions and water levels, as well as any dangers like as submerged logs or rocks.

In summary, kayaking and canoeing are popular outdoor sports in Victoria, giving a unique opportunity to explore the state's rivers and stunning landscapes. Both hobbies demand strong physical fitness, balance, and coordination, as well as respect to safety norms and laws.

• HOT AIR BALOONING

Hot air ballooning is a popular and thrilling hobby that includes soaring in a balloon to experience the spectacular views from above. It's a unique experience that gives a distinct view of the area and is a terrific way to admire the beauty of Victoria.

Victoria offers various areas where you may experience hot air ballooning, including the Yarra Valley, the Grampians, and the Daylesford and Macedon Ranges. The Yarra Valley, in particular, is a popular destination for hot air ballooning because to its gorgeous landscape and perfect weather conditions.

A normal hot air balloon flight starts early in the morning, generally before sunrise. You will meet your pilot and crew, who will take you through a safety briefing before taking off. Once you're in the balloon, you'll gently climb into the sky, taking in the breathtaking views of the surrounding landscape.

As you glide softly through the terrain, you'll have the opportunity to take in the grandeur of the surroundings from a unique viewpoint. You may witness vineyards, mountains, woods, and wildlife as you soar above the treetops.

Many hot air balloon excursions include a glass of champagne or a little breakfast on landing, making it a memorable experience.

Hot air ballooning is a safe and serene pastime, appropriate for individuals of all ages and fitness levels. Most operators have skilled pilots who are certified and qualified to fly hot air balloons.

It's crucial to verify with your operator to ensure that they have the required safety precautions in place and are accredited by the relevant regulatory bodies.

- **WILDLIFE SAFARI**

A wildlife safari is an exciting trip that allows you to observe the natural splendor of Victoria's animals up close. Victoria is home to a range of distinct and diverse animal species, many of which may be witnessed in their native settings on wildlife safaris.

One of the most famous wildlife safari spots in Victoria is the Great Ocean Road. Here, tourists may view koalas, kangaroos, wallabies, echidnas, and a variety of bird species along the rough shoreline and in the neighboring woodlands.

Another popular wildlife safari site is the Grampians National Park. Visitors may witness kangaroos, wallabies, emus, and a variety of bird species on guided excursions of the park. The Grampians is also home to a huge population of eastern grey kangaroos, which may be clearly recognized at dawn and night.

The Phillip Island Nature Park is another popular place for wildlife safaris in Victoria. Here, tourists may see the world-famous penguin parade, as hundreds of tiny penguins emerge from the water and waddle across the beach to their burrows. The park is also home to a huge colony of fur seals, which may be seen on guided boat cruises.

The Wilsons Promontory National Park is another wildlife safari site that offers a unique experience. Here, visitors may view wombats, wallabies, kangaroos, and a variety of bird species on guided walks through the park's lush woodlands and grasslands.

In addition to these renowned places, Victoria also provides a range of wildlife safaris that appeal to diverse interests and tastes. Whether you're interested in bird watching, photography, or simply immersing yourself in nature, there's a wildlife safari in Victoria that's suitable for you.

It's vital to note that while wildlife safaris give an opportunity to watch animals in their natural habitats, it's crucial to always respect the animals and their surroundings.

Visitors should follow all safety recommendations and laws, and should never feed or touch the animals. By doing so, we help guarantee that these lovely species stay protected and continue to thrive in their natural habitats for decades to come.

SHOPPING AND DINING IN MELBOURNE

Melbourne is recognized for its lively eating scene and distinctive shopping experience. With a number of alternatives to pick from, it can be hard to know where to start. Here are some of the top locations to shop and dine in Melbourne.

- **SHOPPING**

Queen Victoria Market: One of Melbourne's famous attractions, this historic market provides a large assortment of fresh vegetables, specialty delicacies, and distinctive gifts. It is an excellent spot to sample local produce and get a sense for the city's food culture.

Collins Street: This street is home to some of the world's most premium brands such as Louis Vuitton, Prada, and Gucci. The architecture of the buildings is also a feature, with many antique structures still surviving.

Chapel Street: This busy street is famed for its chic boutiques, vintage businesses, and eccentric eateries. It is a terrific site to get unusual apparel and accessories.

Bourke Street Mall: This is Melbourne's primary retail zone, including a mix of department stores, speciality shops, and eateries. It is a popular place for residents and visitors alike.

- **DINING**

Chinatown: Located in the center of the city, Chinatown provides a selection of authentic Chinese food. Dumplings, noodles, and roast duck are among the popular foods to sample.

Lygon Street: Also known as "Little Italy," Lygon Street is home to some of the top Italian restaurants in Melbourne. From basic pizzas to handmade pastas, there is something for everyone.

Hardware Lane: This alley is dotted with restaurants and cafés, offering a diversity of cuisines from across the world. It is a popular venue for breakfast and lunch.

Fitzroy: This neighborhood is recognized for its fashionable cafés, pubs, and restaurants. It is a terrific spot to explore if you're searching for something a little more unusual and off-the-beaten-path.

St Kilda: This coastal area is a popular location for visitors and residents alike. There are many restaurants and cafés to pick from, with many having spectacular views of the ocean.

In summary, Melbourne provides a diversified shopping and dining experience that appeals to all interests and inclinations. From high-end luxury boutiques to real ethnic food, there is something for everyone to enjoy.

MELBOURNE'S NIGHTLIFE

Melbourne is widely recognized for its bustling and diverse nightlife, with plenty to offer for everyone, whether you're into live music, comedy, theater, or simply a night out with friends. The city's nightlife scene is centered on the central business district (CBD) and the adjacent inner suburbs.

One of the most popular spots for nightlife in Melbourne is the laneways of the CBD. These small lanes are home to a range of restaurants and clubs, from fashionable cocktail bars to subterranean nightclubs.

Some of the more popular laneway bars are Eau de Vie, a refined speakeasy-style bar, and

Section 8, a laid-back outdoor pub fashioned from shipping containers.

If you're seeking for live music, Melbourne boasts a booming music scene, with a selection of venues catering to all genres. The Tote in Collingwood is a famed rock venue, while the Corner Hotel in Richmond welcomes everything from indie bands to techno performers. For jazz fans, the Paris Cat Jazz Club in the CBD is a must-visit.

Melbourne is also home to a strong comedy industry, with a selection of comedy clubs and events around the city. The Comedy Theatre in the CBD produces regular events, while the Comics Lounge in North Melbourne is a popular place for up-and-coming comedians.

For those searching for a more upmarket nightlife experience, Melbourne boasts dozens of high-end clubs and rooftop locations. The Rooftop Bar in the CBD gives amazing views of the city skyline, while Siglo Bar, located on top of the Melbourne Supper Club, is a refined setting for a cocktail or bottle of wine.

Foodies will also find lots to adore in Melbourne's nightlife scene, with a choice of late-night food options accessible around the city. Chinatown in the CBD is home to some of Melbourne's greatest Asian cuisine, while the Queen Victoria Market features a selection of culinary booths and merchants.

CHAPTER FOUR

QUEENSLAND AND GREAT BARRIER REEF

Queensland, located in the northeast section of Australia, is noted for its tropical climate, magnificent beaches, and unusual biodiversity. It is the second-largest state in Australia, with an area of nearly 1.7 million square kilometers.

One of the most prominent attractions in Queensland is the Great Barrier Reef, which is the world's biggest coral reef system and a UNESCO World Heritage Site. The reef is home to a wealth of marine life, including over 1,500 kinds of fish, and attracts millions of people from across the world each year.

In addition to the Great Barrier Reef, Queensland provides a range of other natural treasures, including rainforests, waterfalls, and national parks. The state is also home to lively cities, such as Brisbane and the Gold Coast, which provide a range of cultural, gastronomic, and entertainment experiences.

With its varied selection of attractions, Queensland is a popular location for travelers seeking adventure, leisure, and a distinct Australian experience.

TOP ATTRACTIONS

- ## THE GREAT BARRIER

The Great Barrier Reef is one of the most spectacular natural marvels in the world and is one of Australia's most popular tourist attractions. It is located in the Coral Sea, off the coast of Queensland, and extends over 2,300 kilometers.

The Great Barrier Reef is made up of thousands of distinct reefs and hundreds of islands, and is home to an astonishing diversity of marine life, including over 1,500 kinds of fish, six species of sea turtles, and a variety of sharks, dolphins, and whales.

The Great Barrier Reef is a refuge for diving and snorkeling aficionados, who travel from all over the globe to explore the reef's crystal-clear waters and marvel at the colorful coral gardens and rich marine life.

There are many various ways to explore the Great Barrier Reef, from snorkeling excursions and glass-bottom boat rides to diving adventures and spectacular helicopter flights.

One of the most popular activities on the Great Barrier Reef is scuba diving. With more than 1,000 dive sites to select from, divers may explore a range of varied settings, from shallow coral gardens to deep marine tunnels.

The Great Barrier Reef is also home to many shipwrecks, offering divers the opportunity to investigate underwater history.

For those who prefer to stay above water, there are numerous additional things to enjoy on the Great Barrier Reef. Glass-bottom boat excursions give a unique viewpoint on the reef, allowing tourists to witness the magnificent marine life without getting wet.

Snorkeling is also a popular pastime, with several tour operators providing equipment and guides to assist guests discover the finest locations.

Aside from aquatic life, the Great Barrier Reef also features several lovely islands and beaches. Some of the most popular include Green Island, Fitzroy Island, and Hamilton Island, each having their distinct attractions and activities.

Visitors may relax on the beaches, explore the islands on foot, or take part in sports like kayaking, paddleboarding, and jet skiing.

Despite its appeal as a tourist attraction, the Great Barrier Reef is under serious risks from climate change, pollution, and other environmental concerns. Conservation initiatives are ongoing to conserve this wonderful natural beauty for future generations to enjoy.

The Great Barrier Reef is a fantastic site that allows tourists the chance to witness the beauty and diversity of the undersea environment. With so much to see and do, it's little wonder that it is regarded as one of the world's greatest natural marvels.

THE GREAT BARRIER REEF

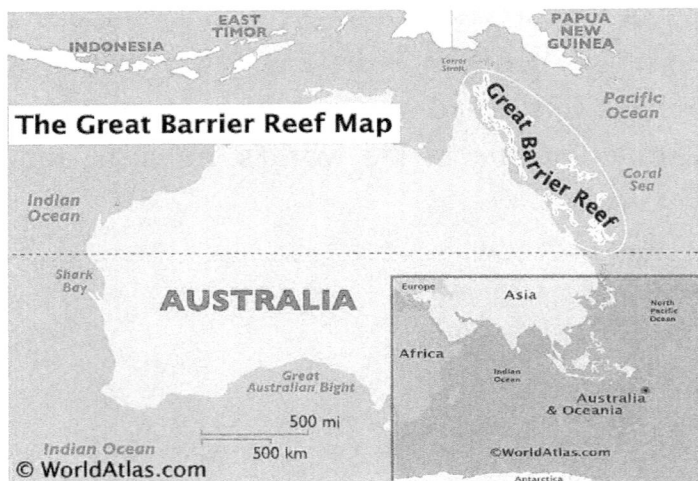

The Great Barrier Reef Map

• DAIBTREE RAINFOREST

The Daintree Rainforest is located in Queensland, Australia, and is one of the most ancient rainforests in the world. It is about 135 million years old and is one of the few surviving rainforests in the world that is intact in its natural condition.

The Daintree Rainforest encompasses an area of roughly 1,200 square kilometers and is home to some of the most unusual and diverse plant and animal species on the globe.

The Daintree Rainforest is a World Heritage Site, and its ecology is regarded to be one of the most complex and diversified on earth. The forest is home to approximately 430 bird species, 12,000 insect species, and 13 distinct types of reptiles.

It is also home to approximately 18,000 plant species, many of which are found nowhere else in the world.

Visitors to the Daintree Rainforest can join a guided tour to learn about the flora and animals of the region. The excursions are generally performed by professional guides who will offer guests thorough information about the flora and creatures that dwell in the rainforest.

Visitors may also take a stroll along one of the several walking paths in the region, which range from simple to strenuous, depending on the visitor's degree of fitness.

One of the most popular activities in the Daintree Rainforest is exploring the Mossman Gorge. The gorge is a wonderful and serene spot, with crystal clear waterways, rich flora, and spectacular views.

Visitors may swim in the gorge's natural swimming holes, take a refreshing plunge in the river, or simply relax on the rocks and take in the gorgeous surroundings.

Another popular attraction in the Daintree Rainforest is the Daintree Discovery Centre. The site provides visitors the ability to learn about the ecology of the rainforest through interactive exhibits and displays.

Visitors may also take a guided tour of the center's boardwalks and learn about the numerous varieties of plants and animals that dwell in the rainforest.

In addition to these activities, tourists may also enjoy a picturesque drive over the Bloomfield Track, a steep and demanding route that weaves its way through the rain.

• WHITSUNDAY ISLAND

Whitsunday Island is a picturesque and renowned location located in the center of the

Whitsunday Islands, Queensland, Australia. It is a prominent tourist attraction that attracts millions of people every year, owing to its amazing natural beauty, crystal clear seas, and white sandy beaches.

The island is the largest of the 74 islands in the Whitsunday area and is famed for its stunning beaches, notably the world-famous Whitehaven Beach.

The beach spans for nearly seven kilometres, with immaculate white silica sand and crystal-clear blue water. It's one of the most photographed beaches in Australia and is consistently ranked one of the finest beaches in the world.

Apart from Whitehaven Beach, other prominent attractions on Whitsunday Island include Hill Inlet, where tourists may take a guided tour and witness the spectacular views of the island's turquoise seas and the surrounding forest from the viewpoint.

Visitors may also explore the island's tropical rainforests and discover some of the unusual flora and fauna species that call the island home.

For those who prefer water sports, the island provides a choice of activities such as snorkelling, scuba diving, and swimming. Visitors may also take a trip around the island or embark on a sailing experience.

Fishing is also a popular sport on Whitsunday Island, with the island's seas overflowing with many varieties of fish.

Whitsunday Island is also home to many lodging alternatives, ranging from opulent resorts to camping sites. It's the perfect place for families, couples, and single travellers wishing to explore the natural beauty of Australia's coastline.

With its gorgeous scenery, crystal-clear oceans, and plenty of activities, Whitsunday Island is a must-visit location for anybody traveling the Great Barrier Reef and Queensland region.

• GOLD COAST

The Gold Coast is a seaside city located in the southeastern section of Queensland, Australia. It spans for over 70 kilometers along the shore of the Pacific Ocean and is recognized for its magnificent beaches, vibrant atmosphere, and many entertainment alternatives. It is a popular resort for travelers, especially those searching for sun, sand, and sea.

One of the biggest attractions of the Gold Coast is its magnificent beaches. The coastline is home to numerous notable beaches like as Surfers Paradise, Main Beach, Broadbeach, Burleigh Heads, and Coolangatta.

The beaches are famed for their white sand, crystal-clear seas, and outstanding surf conditions. Many of the beaches are monitored by lifeguards, making them safe for swimming and other water sports.

Apart from the beaches, the Gold Coast is also home to various theme parks, which are great for family amusement. Dreamworld is one of the most popular theme parks on the Gold Coast and provides a number of rides and attractions, including the Tower of Terror II, the Giant Drop, and the Wipeout. Other theme parks include Sea World, Wet 'n' Wild, and Movie World.

Another draw of the Gold Coast is its shopping and eating options. The city includes a number of shopping malls, including Pacific Fair, Harbour Town, and Robina Town Centre, which provide a wide selection of fashion, cosmetics, and homewares businesses. The eating options on the Gold Coast are likewise diversified, with a selection of eateries providing local and foreign cuisine.

For people interested in environment and animals, the Gold Coast provides a choice of activities, such as whale watching, wildlife sanctuaries, and national parks.

Currumbin Wildlife Sanctuary is a popular location, where tourists may interact with wildlife such as koalas, kangaroos, and crocodiles. The Gold Coast Hinterland is also home to numerous national parks, including Lamington National Park and Springbrook National Park, which provide hiking trails, waterfalls, and breathtaking vistas.

In terms of nightlife, the Gold Coast boasts a choice of pubs, clubs, and entertainment alternatives. Surfers Paradise is famed for its nightlife, with several pubs and clubs lining the streets. The Star Gold Coast is also a prominent entertainment center, featuring a range of performances, concerts, and events.

The Gold Coast is a bustling and exciting location that provides something for everyone, whether you are seeking for sun, sand, and surf, family entertainment, shopping, cuisine, wildlife, or nightlife.

- **FRASER ISLAND**

Fraser Island is the world's biggest sand island, located off the southeastern coast of Queensland, Australia. The island is around 120 kilometers long and spans an area of approximately 184,000 hectares.

Fraser Island is noted for its distinctive natural beauty and diversified ecosystems, which include rainforests, freshwater lakes, sand dunes, and mangrove forests.

The island is a popular destination for travelers, offering a multitude of activities and attractions. Visitors may explore the island via 4WD vehicle or on foot, with several guided trips available.

One of the most prominent attractions of Fraser Island is the freshwater lakes, such as Lake

McKenzie, which is famed for its crystal blue water and white sand beaches. Other popular lakes are Lake Wabby and Lake Birrabeen.

Fraser Island is also home to various types of fauna, including dingoes, wallabies, and several species of birds. Visitors are cautioned to remain cautious around dingoes and to respect the island's stringent guidelines for contact with them.

One of the distinctive aspects of Fraser Island is the existence of the Maheno Shipwreck, which washed ashore in 1935 and has become a renowned tourist destination. The island is also home to various historic sites, including the ruins of a World War II radar station.

For those seeking adventure, Fraser Island provides a multitude of activities, such as hiking, camping, and sandboarding. The island's sand dunes are famous for sandboarding, and tourists may also enjoy guided excursions through the island's rainforests and along its beaches.

Accommodation on Fraser Island ranges from camping and backpacker hostels to luxury resorts. Visitors can pick from a number of alternatives, based on their budget and tastes .

- **KURANDA SCENIC RAILWAY**

The Kuranda Scenic Railway is a renowned tourist destination in Queensland, Australia. The railway is a historic train route that connects the seaside town of Cairns to the mountain village of Kuranda, bringing passengers on a spectacular ride through the lush tropical rainforest of Far North Queensland.

The railway was built almost 120 years ago in the late 1800s and early 1900s by a crew of 1500 men who had to cut out tunnels and bridges through the steep terrain of the Barron Gorge National Park.

Today, the Kuranda Scenic Railway has become one of the most prominent tourist attractions in the region, pulling in people from all over the world who come to see the breathtaking vistas of the rainforest and the Barron Falls.

The Kuranda Scenic Railway offers a unique and fascinating ride through the rainforest, presenting guests with panoramic views of the tropical terrain and the fauna that inhabits it.

The train trip takes around 90 minutes, snaking through the jungle, through cascading waterfalls, and over towering bridges, presenting passengers with spectacular views at every turn.

Visitors can pick from a range of ticket options, including the normal service, gold class service, and diamond class service. The base service comprises a one-way journey on the Kuranda Scenic Railway, while the gold and diamond class services provide superior seats, complimentary drinks, and access to unique observation platforms.

In addition to the train trip, guests may also explore the hamlet of Kuranda, which provides a selection of unique activities and experiences. The hamlet is home to a variety of local craftsmen and crafters, as well as various stores, restaurants, and cafes. Visitors may also visit the nearby animal parks, including the Kuranda Koala Gardens, the Australian Butterfly Sanctuary, and the Rainforestation Nature Park.

- **CAIRNS**

Cairns is a bustling city located in Far North Queensland, Australia. It is a popular location among travelers from throughout the world, receiving millions of people every year. Known for its tropical warmth, gorgeous scenery, and a wealth of activities and attractions, Cairns has something for everyone.

One of the biggest attractions of Cairns is the Great Barrier Reef, which is easily accessible from the city. Visitors may take a boat cruise to the reef to enjoy snorkeling, scuba diving, and other water sports. In addition to the reef, Cairns is also recognized for its magnificent beaches, lush rainforests, and rich fauna.

For visitors searching for a cultural experience, Cairns features various art galleries, museums, and cultural institutions. The Cairns Regional Gallery is a must-visit for art fans, presenting an exceptional collection of both modern and traditional Australian art.

The Tjapukai Aboriginal Cultural Park is another popular location, allowing tourists an opportunity to learn about the local indigenous culture.

In terms of outdoor activities, Cairns has lots to offer. The city is bordered by beautiful rainforests and is home to various environmental parks and reserves. Visitors may take a stroll in the Daintree Rainforest, explore the Barron

Gorge National Park, or take a picturesque drive to the adjacent Atherton Tablelands.

Cairns also offers a thriving nighttime culture, with a range of pubs, clubs, and restaurants to pick from. Visitors may enjoy a refreshing drink at one of the city's numerous bars, dance the night away at a nightclub, or sample some of the great local food at one of the many restaurants.

SNORKELING AND DIVING IN THE GREAT BARRIER REEF

Snorkeling and diving are popular activities at the Great Barrier Reef as they allow tourists to experience the underwater environment of the reef up close. Snorkeling is a simple and accessible method to view the reef, and it takes minimum equipment. Visitors may snorkel from a boat or from the shore, and many excursions and packages offer snorkeling gear as part of the experience.

Diving is a more immersive way to explore the reef, and there are several dive companies that provide a range of activities for all skill levels. Certified divers may take part in guided dives or join multi-day liveaboard expeditions, where they can dive in some of the most isolated and pristine regions of the reef.

One of the most popular regions for snorkeling and diving in the Great Barrier Reef is the Cairns region, which is home to a variety of spectacular coral cays and reefs. Green Island and Fitzroy Island are popular destinations for day excursions from Cairns, and guests may snorkel or dive from the shore or join a boat tour to explore the surrounding reefs.

Further north, the ribbon reefs and coral gardens of the Outer Great Barrier Reef provide some of the greatest diving and snorkeling experiences in the world. Visitors may observe colorful fish, turtles, sharks, and other marine species as they explore the crystal-clear waters of the reef.

It is crucial to highlight that while snorkeling and diving are amazing experiences, it is important to be aware of the possible hazards and take required measures. Visitors should always heed to the recommendations of their tour operators, wear adequate safety gear, and avoid touching or disturbing the fragile coral and aquatic life.

BEST PLACES TO SHOP AND DINE IN QUEENSLAND

Queensland is a state in Australia that has a lot to offer in terms of shopping and eating experiences. From small, boutique shops to major shopping areas, there is something for everyone. In addition, there is a wide range of dining alternatives accessible, from high-end restaurants to informal cafés and street food sellers. Here are some of the top locations to shop and dine in Queensland:

Queen Street Mall: Located in Brisbane, the Queen Street Mall is a pedestrian mall that is home to over 700 merchants, including department stores, boutique shops, and restaurants. It is the best spot to get anything from high-end apparel to unusual gifts.

Pacific Fair retail Centre: Located near the Gold Coast, Pacific Fair is one of the major retail malls in Queensland, with over 400 businesses. The mall features a wide selection of merchants, from high-end names to budget fashion boutiques, as well as a theater and several food options.

Noosa Junction: Noosa Junction is a bustling shopping and dining complex located in the seaside resort of Noosa. The region is home to a selection of boutique stores, cafés, and restaurants, with a focus on local and ecological products.

James Street: Located in Fortitude Valley, Brisbane, James Street is a busy retail and dining destination that is noted for its fashion shops, homeware businesses, and cafés. The region has a casual, bohemian air and is popular with residents and visitors alike.

Eat Street Northshore: This popular food market is located in Hamilton, Brisbane, and is open every Saturday. It provides a wide choice of foreign street cuisine, live music, and a casual ambiance.

Broadbeach: Located on the Gold Coast, Broadbeach is a popular eating destination that is home to several restaurants, cafés, and pubs. The neighborhood has a laid-back atmosphere and is excellent for sharing a meal or a drink with friends.

Portside Wharf: Located in Hamilton, Brisbane, Portside Wharf is a contemporary complex that offers a choice of food and shopping opportunities. It is also a popular site for gatherings and boasts a gorgeous waterfront position.

Hastings Street: Located in Noosa, Hastings Street is a lively shopping and dining sector that is popular with tourists. The region is home to various cafés, restaurants, and boutique stores, as well as a gorgeous beach.

NIGHTLIFE IN QUEENSLAND

Queensland is home to some of the most dynamic nightlife scenes in Australia, with an assortment of pubs, nightclubs, and entertainment venues located throughout the state.

From the busy streets of Brisbane to the seaside communities of the Gold Coast, there's something for everyone when it comes to Queensland nightlife.

Brisbane is the state's capital city and features a lively nightlife scene. Fortitude Valley is one of the best-known places for nightlife in Brisbane, with a large choice of pubs, clubs, and live music venues on offer.

The Tivoli, located in Fortitude Valley, is one of Brisbane's most renowned live music venues and has featured some of the greatest names in music.

The Gold Coast is another favorite location for visitors wanting a night out. Surfers Paradise is the center of the Gold Coast's nightlife, with an abundance of pubs, nightclubs, and restaurants along the streets.

Elsewhere on the Gold Coast, Broadbeach is another popular location for people seeking for a night out, with a choice of pubs, clubs, and restaurants on offer.

Cairns is another popular location for visitors seeking nightlife in Queensland. The city is home to a number of pubs and nightclubs, with Rusty's Markets having a more laid-back, informal vibe. For those seeking to dance the night away, The Woolshed is one of Cairns' most popular nightclubs.

The Sunshine Coast is also a wonderful area to enjoy Queensland's nightlife culture, with the seaside towns of Mooloolaba and Noosa providing an assortment of pubs, clubs, and restaurants.

The Wharf Mooloolaba is a popular area for visitors wishing to have a drink by the ocean, while Hastings Street in Noosa is crowded with restaurants and pubs.

In addition to the conventional nightlife scene, Queensland also provides a choice of cultural events and festivals throughout the year. From the Brisbane Festival to the Gold Coast's Blues on Broadbeach, there's always something going on in Queensland.

THE CULTURAL EVENTS AND FESTIVALS IN QUEENSLAND

Queensland is home to many distinct cultures and groups, and as a result, there are several cultural events and festivals throughout the year. These events are a terrific chance to explore the distinct customs, music, art, and food of the state and its people.

One of the greatest cultural events in Queensland is the Cairns Indigenous Art Fair. This event, which takes place in Cairns, celebrates the work of some of the state's most brilliant Aboriginal and Torres Strait Islander artists. Visitors may purchase art, attend seminars, and see performances by traditional dancers and musicians.

Another popular cultural festival is the Woodford Folk Festival, which takes place every year on the Sunshine Coast Hinterland. This festival involves more than 2000 performers, including musicians, artists, and poets, and attracts thousands of people from all over the world.

The festival highlights the richness of Australian culture and involves performances from many different cultural groups, including Indigenous Australians, African Australians, and Pacific Islanders.

The Brisbane Festival is another prominent cultural event in Queensland. This festival takes place in September and comprises a wide range of events, including theater plays, music concerts, and art exhibitions.

The event attracts both local and international artists and performers and is a celebration of the thriving cultural landscape in Brisbane.

Queensland is also home to various cultural events honoring its agricultural past. The EKKA, or Royal Queensland Show, is one of the major agricultural events in the country and is held in August in Brisbane.

The festival incorporates animal displays, contests, and exhibits exhibiting the state's agricultural goods and customs.

Other popular cultural events in Queensland include the Noosa Food and Wine Festival, the Gold Coast Film Festival, and the Australian Surfing Festival. Whatever your hobbies, there is bound to be a cultural event or festival in Queensland that will appeal to you.

CHAPTER FIVE

THE NORTHERN TERRITORY AND THE OUTBACK

The Northern Territory is a vast region located in the central-northern part of Australia, covering an area of over 1.4 million square kilometers. The region is characterized by vast stretches of wilderness and some of the most rugged and remote landscapes on earth.

The Northern Territory is home to a diverse range of natural wonders, including the iconic Uluru (Ayers Rock), Kakadu National Park, and the MacDonnell Ranges. The region is also home to a rich cultural heritage, with strong connections to the Aboriginal peoples of Australia.

The Northern Territory is known for its rugged and remote landscapes, which have inspired writers, artists, and filmmakers for generations.

The region is also known for its vibrant Aboriginal culture, which has been preserved through the centuries in rock art, storytelling, and dance.

Visitors to the Northern Territory can experience the unique and ancient cultures of the region's indigenous peoples, as well as exploring the natural wonders of the Outback, such as towering red rock formations, vast canyons, and stunning waterfalls.

The Northern Territory is also home to a number of unique and fascinating communities, each with their own distinct cultural traditions and ways of life.

These communities include the Tiwi Islands, located off the coast of Darwin, which are renowned for their art, music, and dance; and the communities of the Western Desert, where visitors can learn about the ancient traditions of the Pintupi people and other desert-dwelling Aboriginal groups.

TOP ATTRACTIONS IN THE NORTHERN TERRITORY AND THE OUTBACK

The Northern Territory and the Outback are known for their stunning natural landscapes, unique wildlife, and rich cultural heritage. Here are some of the top attractions to explore:

- **ULURU (AYERS ROCK)**

Uluru, commonly known as Ayers Rock, is one of the most recognizable sites in Australia and is located in the Northern Territory. This enormous sandstone monolith is important to the local Indigenous Anangu people, who have lived in the area for tens of thousands of years. Uluru is a UNESCO World Heritage Site that attracts thousands of visitors each year.

One of the most remarkable aspects about Uluru is its immensity. It rises at 348 meters (1,142 feet) tall and has a diameter of 9.4 kilometers (5.8 miles). The rock itself is formed of arkose, a kind of sandstone that has a characteristic red hue.

One of the most popular activities in Uluru is to watch the sunset or dawn over the rock. Visitors may watch this spectacular spectacle from a designated viewing area, or by joining a guided tour that gives a more immersive experience. The shifting hues of the rock as the sun moves across the sky are incredibly magnificent and allow for some fantastic photo opportunity.

Another popular activity in Uluru is to take a guided tour of the base of the rock. These trips are given by Indigenous leaders who share their expertise of the area's history, culture, and spiritual importance. Visitors can also take a guided excursion to the adjacent Kata Tjuta rock formations, which are equally important to the Anangu people.

Uluru-Kata Tjuta National Park, where Uluru is located, offers a choice of lodging alternatives for guests, including camping sites, motels, and luxury lodges. Visitors may also enjoy a number of activities such as bushwalking, birding, and star-gazing.

It's vital to note that Uluru is a sacred location for the Anangu people and tourists are urged to respect their culture and practices while visiting. The park also has tight laws regulating the climbing of Uluru, which is forbidden owing to safety concerns and the cultural significance of the place.

• KAKADU NATIONAL PARK

Kakadu National Park is a huge protected area located in the Northern Territory of Australia. It is a site of extraordinary natural beauty and cultural value, encompassing over 20,000 square kilometers. The park is a UNESCO World Heritage Site, recognized for both its ecological and cultural value.

Kakadu is home to an astonishing mix of flora and wildlife, including more than 280 bird species, 60 species of animal, and 10,000 types of insects. The park is also noted for its diversified scenery, which includes rivers, marshes, savannah woods, and rocky sandstone cliffs.

This unusual ecosystem provides a home for a broad range of animals, including some of Australia's most iconic species, such as saltwater crocodiles, wallabies, and kangaroos.

One of the most stunning elements of Kakadu is its wetlands. The park's floodplains and billabongs are home to a wide assortment of birds, including magpie geese, whistling ducks, and the rare jabiru. Visitors can take guided tours of the wetlands or explore them alone by canoe or boat. The park's waterways also give a wonderful chance for fishing and swimming.

Kakadu is also home to some of the most significant rock art sites in the world. The rock art in Kakadu stretches back over 20,000 years and gives an insight into the cultural past of the area's Aboriginal inhabitants.

The park includes a number of guided tours and excursions that allow guests to explore these places and learn about the significance of the art.

Other popular activities in Kakadu include bushwalking, camping, and 4WD trips. The park features a number of walking pathways that appeal to all levels of fitness and expertise. Visitors can also camp in the park, either in established campgrounds or in isolated locations with a permission.

- **KINGS CANYON**

Kings Canyon is a magnificent sandstone canyon found in Watarrka National Park in the Northern Territory of Australia. The canyon is located around 300 km southwest of Alice Springs and is a popular location for nature aficionados and adventure seekers.

The canyon is formed by the Kings Creek, which has carved through the sandstone over millions of years, forming a steep valley that is over 270 meters deep in some sections. The walls of the canyon are tall and have a reddish tint that contrasts well with the blue sky.

One of the most popular things to do at Kings Canyon is to trek the Rim Walk, which is a six-kilometer circle that takes you around the edge of the canyon.

The walk provides beautiful views of the canyon, including the Garden of Eden, a natural paradise that is tucked in the canyon floor. The hike is considered tough and takes roughly three to four hours to finish, depending on your level of fitness.

Another popular hike is the Kings Creek trip, which is a two-kilometer return trip that brings you to the canyon floor. The walk leads you through thick greenery, and you may view a variety of wildlife and reptiles along the way. The hike is rated simple and takes roughly one hour to complete.

For those who want a more leisurely experience, Kings Canyon provides helicopter tours that provide stunning aerial views of the canyon and the surrounding environment. The flights are conducted by expert pilots and give a unique perspective of the canyon that you can't obtain from the ground.

In addition to hiking and helicopter excursions, Kings Canyon provides a number of other activities, including quad bike tours, camel rides, and scenic drives. There is also a cultural center that offers educational events and displays that promote the indigenous history and culture of the area.

Kings Canyon is a wonderfully spectacular natural marvel that should not be missed by anybody visiting to the Northern Territory. With its towering sandstone cliffs, rich flora, and crystal-clear waterholes, Kings Canyon is a must-visit location for nature aficionados and adventure seekers.

- **ALICE SPRINGS**

Alice Springs is a dynamic and distinctive town nestled in the heart of the Australian Outback in the Northern Territory. It is situated in a spectacular desert terrain and is noted for its rich Aboriginal culture, stunning natural features, and interesting history.

One of the primary attractions of Alice Springs is the Alice Springs Desert Park, which is a good site to learn about the local flora and animals.

Visitors may enjoy a number of interactive exhibits and events, including the nocturnal home, where you can witness native species that only come out at night. There is also a bird of prey display where you may watch spectacular birds in flight.

Another must-visit item in Alice Springs is the Royal Flying Doctor Service, which is a museum that highlights the history of the service that provides medical treatment to people in remote regions of Australia.

Visitors may learn about the wonderful job that the organization conducts, as well as witness the planes that are used to transfer patients.

The Alice Springs Telegraph Station Historical Reserve is another intriguing destination that gives insights into the town's early past. The station was the site of the first telegraph station in the area and was an essential element of the communication network that connected Australia to the rest of the globe. Visitors may visit the historic buildings, see the museum, and join a guided tour to learn about the station's history.

In addition to these attractions, Alice Springs is also an excellent base for visiting the surrounding areas, notably the West MacDonnell Ranges, which provide some of the most stunning scenery in the region.

Visitors may enjoy a stroll along the Larapinta Trail, which offers spectacular views of the surrounding mountains, canyons, and waterholes. The adjacent Alice Springs Golf Club is also a popular attraction, featuring a difficult course situated in a gorgeous desert terrain.

- **KATHERINE GEORGE**

Katherine Gorge is a sequence of thirteen sandstone gorges found in the Nitmiluk National Park, Northern Territory, Australia. It is situated roughly 244 kilometers southeast of Darwin and 30 km northeast of Katherine. The gorge system is located on the grounds of the Jawoyn people, who are the traditional proprietors of this region.

The term Nitmiluk is the Jawoyn name for the area which means "place of the cicada dreaming". The gorge system is a component of the greater Katherine River system and it is one of the most popular tourist sites in the Northern Territory.

The Katherine Gorge system is a natural wonder that highlights the beauty and diversity of the Australian outback. It is made up of thirteen different gorges, each with its unique qualities, from towering sandstone cliffs to crystal blue streams.

Visitors may explore the gorges by boat or on foot, with guided tours available for those who wish to learn more about the area's history and ecology.

One of the pleasures of a visit to Katherine valley is a cruise along the river, which gives guests with breathtaking views of the towering sandstone cliffs and an opportunity to observe the natural fauna that calls the valley home.

Visitors may also join a guided tour of the region, where they can learn about the original owners of the land, the Jawoyn people, and their culture and history.

Katherine Gorge is also a popular location for hikers and explorers, with various walking paths accessible for tourists of all ability levels. The Jatbula track is a famous 5-day hiking track that takes tourists through the Nitmiluk National Park and along the Katherine River, affording beautiful views of the valley and its surrounds.

The path is well-marked and offers camping amenities along the way, making it a popular location for hikers looking for a more immersive experience.

OUTDOOR ACTIVITIES IN THE NORTHERN TERRITORY AND THE OUTBACK

The Northern Territory and the Outback are recognized for their rough terrain and magnificent natural beauty, making it the perfect location for adventure enthusiasts. From hiking to camping, there are several outdoor activities that visitors may enjoy while visiting this region. Here are some of the top outdoor activities to attempt in the Northern Territory and the Outback:

Hiking and Trekking: The Northern Territory and the Outback are home to numerous amazing hiking and trekking paths, including the Larapinta Trail, the Overland Track, and the Jatbula Trail. These routes provide spectacular views of the region, and tourists may observe animals and local flora and fauna while walking.

Camping: Camping is a terrific opportunity to immerse oneself in the natural surroundings of the Northern Territory and the Outback. There are various campsites in the region, notably at Uluru and Kakadu National Park. Camping allows tourists to appreciate the quiet and tranquility of the environment and watch the stars in the night sky.

Wildlife Safaris: Visitors may go on guided wildlife safaris to observe the classic Australian species, such as kangaroos, wallabies, and dingoes, in their native habitats. The Nitmiluk National Park is an excellent area for wildlife safaris, where tourists may view saltwater crocodiles and bird species like the black kite and the rainbow bee-eater.

Hot Air Ballooning: Hot air ballooning is a unique and thrilling way to experience the Northern Territory and the Outback from a fresh perspective. Visitors may enjoy a hot air balloon flight over the region's natural beauties, such as the MacDonnell Ranges and Alice Springs.

Rock Climbing: For adventure enthusiasts, rock climbing is an exciting outdoor sport to undertake in the Northern Territory and the Outback. The region is home to numerous iconic rock formations, such as Uluru and Kings Canyon, that provide demanding and fascinating climbing experiences.

Camel Riding: Camel riding is a popular pastime in the Northern Territory and the Outback, offering visitors a unique opportunity to experience the region's arid terrain. Visitors may join camel excursions at Uluru and Alice Springs to experience riding a camel and learn about the animal's significance in the region's history and culture.

Fishing: The Northern Territory and the Outback are home to some of the greatest fishing areas in Australia, with the Mary River and Daly River being the most popular. Visitors may catch numerous varieties of fish, such as barramundi and threadfin salmon, while enjoying the calm surroundings.

Swimming and Water Sports: The region includes numerous natural waterholes and springs, including the Mataranka Thermal Pool and Gunlom Falls, which give tourists the perfect chance to cool down and enjoy various water sports activities including swimming, kayaking, and paddleboarding.

NIGHTLIFE IN THE NORTHERN TERRITORY

The Northern Territory and the Outback provide a unique nightlife experience that mixes traditional Australian hospitality with the rough landscape of the region. While there aren't many significant cities in this area, there are still plenty of taverns, pubs, and nightclubs to visit.

One of the most popular venues for nightlife in the Northern Territory is Darwin, the capital city. The city's waterfront area is home to various pubs and restaurants, as well as a lively night market that serves a broad range of food, beverages, and local crafts.

For those searching for a more laid-back ambiance, Alice Springs has a selection of pubs and bars that cater to a more casual population. The Red Centre's desert surroundings provide a unique setting for a night out, with numerous restaurants offering live music and entertainment.

In addition to regular nightlife locations, there are also various unique experiences to be obtained in the Northern Territory and the Outback. One popular choice is to go stargazing in the desert, where the bright sky afford a wonderful view of the Milky Way and other celestial objects.

A sunset camel ride across the red sands of Uluru, with food and beverages is another interesting activity. For those who prefer a more adventurous night out, there are also guided excursions that take guests on night treks into the Outback, allowing them to experience the beauty and mystery of the country after dark.

CHAPTER SIX

WESTERN AUSTRALIA

Western Australia is the biggest state in Australia, having an area of nearly 2.5 million square kilometers. The state is recognized for its rough coastline, gorgeous beaches, wide deserts, magnificent scenery, and rich animals. It is home to several unique natural beauties, including the Pinnacles Desert, Karijini National Park, and the Ningaloo Reef, which is one of the longest fringing coral reefs in the world.

Western Australia is also noted for its rich cultural legacy, with many indigenous communities keeping their customs and way of life. The state's capital, Perth, is a contemporary and energetic city, with a laid-back lifestyle, superb food and shopping options, and a booming arts and cultural scene.

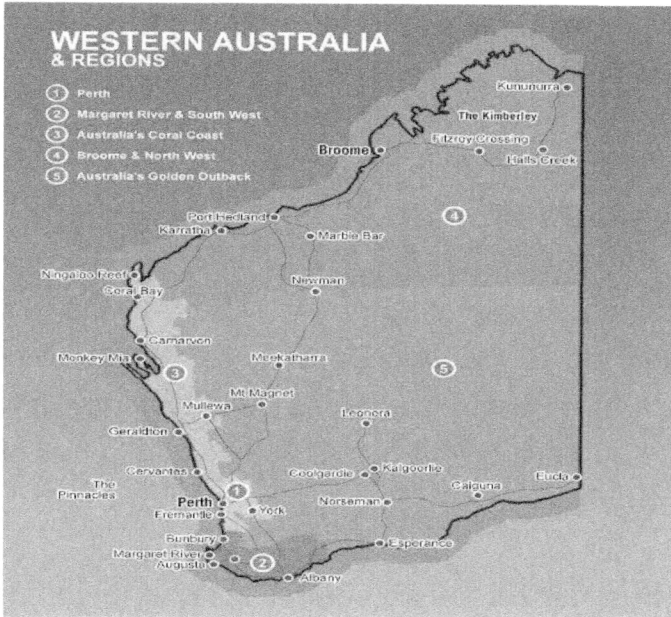

Map of the Western Australia

TOP ATTRACTIONS IN WESTERN AUSTRALIA

- **PERTH**

Perth is the capital city of Western Australia, located on the west coast of Australia. It is the fourth most populated city in Australia and has a reputation as a laid-back, sunny, and dynamic metropolis.

Perth is famed for its natural beauty, including gorgeous beaches, parks, and gardens, as well as its dynamic cultural scene, wonderful food, and busy nightlife.

One of the most popular attractions in Perth is Kings Park, which is located in the heart of the city and has spectacular views of the Swan River and the Perth skyline.

It is one of the largest inner-city parks in the world and offers stunning gardens, walking pathways, picnic spots, playgrounds, and more. Visitors may also enjoy panoramic views of the city from the high walkway, the Lotterywest Federation Walkway.

Another famous destination is the Perth Zoo, located in South Perth. It is home to around 1,200 creatures from across the world, including native Australian species such as kangaroos, koalas, and wombats.

The zoo provides a range of activities, from up-close interactions with animals to behind-the-scenes excursions, and is a terrific location for families to visit.

For anyone interested in history and culture, the Western Australian Museum is a must-visit. It is located in the middle of the city and highlights the natural and cultural heritage of Western Australia. Exhibits span from Aboriginal culture and artifacts to the natural treasures of the state, such as the distinctive flora and animals.

For visitors wishing to enjoy the gorgeous beaches and mild weather, Perth is bordered by wonderful coastal spots, including Cottesloe Beach, Scarborough Beach, and Rottnest Island.

Rottnest Island is a popular day trip location, located just a short boat journey from Perth. It is home to some of the most pristine beaches in the world, as well as a diversity of animals, including the famed quokka.

The Perth Cultural Centre is also a must-visit. It is home to a number of cultural institutions, including the Art Gallery of Western Australia, the State Library of Western Australia, and the Western Australian Performing Arts Centre.

The region also offers a multitude of events throughout the year, from live music and theater performances to art exhibitions and cultural festivals.

• THE MARGARET RIVER REGION

The Margaret River region is a beautiful and popular tourist destination in Western Australia. Located roughly three hours south of Perth, this area is famed for its magnificent beaches, world-class vineyards, gourmet food, and spectacular landscape. With so much to offer, the Margaret River region is a must-visit location for every tourist.

One of the main charms of the Margaret River region is its beaches. There are plenty to pick from, each with its own distinct qualities. Some of the most popular include Surfers Point, Prevelly Beach, and Redgate Beach.

These beaches are wonderful for swimming, surfing, and sunbathing, and are surrounded by gorgeous natural scenery.

In addition to its beaches, the Margaret River region is also home to several vineyards. The area is famed for producing some of the greatest wines in the world, including chardonnay, cabernet sauvignon, and shiraz.

Visitors may take wine tours and tastings, as well as eat wonderful meals at the numerous gourmet restaurants and cafés in the region.

The Margaret River area is also noted for its natural beauty. The region is surrounded by lush woods, rolling hills, and gorgeous streams, making it a perfect place for hiking, cycling, and exploring.

There are numerous national parks and natural reserves in the vicinity, including Leeuwin-Naturaliste National Park, Boranup Forest, and Cape to Cape Track.

For those interested in culture and history, the Margaret River region also has plenty to offer. The area has a strong Aboriginal past, and tourists may learn about the local culture and traditions at several cultural institutions and museums. Additionally, the area boasts a strong arts and crafts industry, with several galleries and studios showing the work of local artists and craftspeople.

• NINGALOO REEF

Ningaloo Reef is a World Heritage-listed location located on the western coast of Australia in the state of Western Australia. It is a large coral reef running over 260 kilometers along the shore of the Ningaloo Coast. The reef is home to a broad diversity of marine life, including over 500 species of fish, hundreds of kinds of coral, and several species of sharks, turtles, and whales.

One of the most fascinating elements of Ningaloo Reef is the possibility to swim alongside whale sharks. These gentle giants, which can grow up to 12 meters in length, pass across the area from April to July each year. Visitors may join a trip to swim with the whale sharks, which is an experience unlike any other.

Another popular activity in Ningaloo Reef is snorkeling and scuba diving. The pristine waters and colorful coral make it a perfect spot for both beginners and expert divers. The reef is accessible from shore in several sections, making it simple to explore.

The Ningaloo Coast is also home to various land-based attractions, including Cape Range National Park. This park includes a harsh terrain with steep gorges, limestone peaks, and sandy beaches. Visitors can explore the park on foot or via four-wheel drive.

Ningaloo Reef Resort

Swimming with shark in the Ningaloo Reef

Another popular destination is Coral Bay, a tiny beach hamlet that provides a range of water sports, including kayaking, paddleboarding, and fishing. Visitors may also take a glass-bottom boat excursion to explore the coral and aquatic life without getting wet.

Broome is a lovely seaside town located in the Kimberley area of Western Australia. Known for its magnificent beaches, rich history, and vibrant culture, Broome is a famous tourist destination that provides a wide choice of sights and activities for tourists to enjoy.

One of the most popular attractions in Broome is the Cable Beach, a spectacular 22 km stretch of immaculate white sand that is regarded as one of the most beautiful beaches in the world. Visitors may enjoy a sunset camel ride down the beach, go for a dip in the crystal-clear seas, or simply relax and soak up the sun.

Another popular attraction in Broome is the town's rich history, which may be studied at the

Broome Historical Museum. The museum has exhibits on the area's pearling business, which was an important part of the local economy in the early 20th century, as well as exhibitions on the town's indigenous culture and early European residents.

For those interested in wildlife, Broome provides various opportunities to get up and personal with some of Australia's most recognizable species. Visitors may join a whale watching cruise during the migration season (June to September), go birding in the Roebuck Bay Bird Observatory, or take a crocodile tour to witness these ancient predators in their natural environment.

Broome is also noted for its distinct ethnic blend, with a dynamic mix of Indigenous Australian, European, and Asian influences. Visitors may experience this cultural richness firsthand by touring the town's various galleries and markets, which showcase a diverse range of indigenous art, handcrafted crafts, and local vegetables.

Broome is a good location for seeing the spectacular Kimberley area, which contains some of Western Australia's most breathtaking natural beauty, including jagged coastline, ancient gorges, and huge, open landscapes. Visitors may take a scenic fly over the area, go on a 4WD excursion to explore some of the region's most isolated locations, or simply relax and enjoy the amazing natural beauty of the area.

- **PURNULULU NATIONAL PARK**

Purnululu National Park, located in the Kimberley area of Western Australia, is a natural marvel that boasts an incredible geological creation known as the Bungle Bungle Range.

The park is notable for its spectacular orange and black striped rock domes that rise up to 578 meters above the surrounding grasslands, producing a remarkable contrast against the clear blue sky.

The Bungle Bungle Range is made up of layers of sandstone that were accumulated over millions of years, which have been worn by wind and water to create the unusual domed formations. The alternate layers of sandstone contain various minerals, which give the rock its characteristic hues.

In addition to the Bungle Bungle number, Purnululu National Park features a number of other natural attractions, including gorges, waterfalls, and pools. One of the most popular sites is Cathedral Gorge, a natural amphitheater with acoustics that make it a popular spot for concerts and events.

The park is also home to a variety of animals, including wallabies, dingoes, and a diverse diversity of bird species. Visitors may experience the park on a choice of guided excursions, from breathtaking helicopter flights above the Bungle Bungle choice to 4WD tours of the area's harsh terrain.

For visitors seeking to remain overnight, there are a number of camping choices available inside the park, from simple campsites to more deluxe glamping alternatives. The best time to visit Purnululu National Park is during the colder months of May to August, when the weather is moderate and dry.

- **ROTTNEST ISLAND**

Rottnest Island is a renowned tourist attraction located 18 kilometers west of the coast of Perth, Western Australia. The island, known locally as "Rotto," is accessible by ferry and provides tourists the opportunity to discover its beautiful beaches, natural beauty, and unusual species.

One of the most popular sports on Rottnest Island is cycling, with the island possessing more than 63 kilometers of bike routes. Visitors may hire bicycles at the ferry station and explore the island at their own speed. The paths provide spectacular views of the coastline, as well as opportunities to see native animals such as quokkas, wallabies, and birds.

Rottnest Island is also home to a variety of stunning beaches, including the famed Pinky Beach, which features crystal-clear water and silky white sand.

Other popular beaches are Geordie Bay, Little Parakeet Bay, and Salmon Bay. Visitors may also enjoy water-based activities such as snorkeling, diving, fishing, and surfing.

One of the island's most prominent sights is the Rottnest Island Lighthouse. The lighthouse, which was completed in 1896, gives beautiful views of the island and the surrounding waters. Visitors can climb the lighthouse's spiral staircase for a panoramic view of the island's harsh scenery.

Rottnest Island is also recognized for its distinctive fauna, with the island being home to the famed quokka, a tiny mammal that has become a prominent tourist attraction. Visitors may often be seen snapping pictures with the gentle critters, which are only located on a few islands off the coast of Western Australia.

For those interested in history, Rottnest Island has a rich cultural past extending back over 40,000 years. The island was a significant place for the Aboriginal Noongar people, and tourists may explore a variety of sites that have cultural value, including the Wadjemup Aboriginal Burial Ground and the Rottnest Island Museum.

- **KARIJINI NATIONAL PARK**

Karijini National Park is a magnificent national park located in the Pilbara area of Western Australia. Covering an area of nearly 6,000 square kilometers, the park is noted for its steep red gorges, waterfalls, and crystal-clear lakes. It is a popular site for hikers, photographers, and environment enthusiasts alike.

One of the primary features of the park is the stunning Karijini Gorge, which is one of the biggest and deepest canyons in Western Australia. The gorge is home to numerous spectacular waterfalls, including the 80-meter-tall Fortescue Falls, which flows into a deep pool that is great for swimming.

Another notable feature of the park is the Hancock Gorge, which is noted for its small canyons, old rock formations, and the picturesque Kermit's Pool. Visitors may climb down into the gorge and enjoy its twisting trails, rock pools, and waterfalls.

Other must-see sites in the park include the Weano Gorge, the Joffre Gorge, and the beautiful Hamersley Range, which is famed for its dramatic red cliffs and stunning vistas.

In addition to its natural beauty, Karijini National Park is also home to various types of fauna, including kangaroos, wallabies, echidnas, and a large variety of bird species. Visitors may also learn about the park's rich cultural past by visiting the neighboring Ngurrangga Tours, which offers guided tours of the local indigenous sites and traditional rock art.

- **SHARK BAY**

Shark Bay is a UNESCO World Heritage Site situated in Western Australia. It is a big and diversified natural harbor with many various ecosystems and geological formations, including some of the world's oldest living fossils.

The region is famous for its abundant marine life, crystal-clear seas, and magnificent natural surroundings.

One of the most prominent attractions in Shark Bay is the Monkey Mia Dolphin Resort, which attracts guests from all over the world. The resort is home to a big pod of bottlenose dolphins, who come into the shallow waters of the bay to socialize with people.

Visitors may witness the dolphins up close as they are fed by park rangers, and even have the option to go into the water and touch them.

Another popular site near Shark Bay is the Francois Peron National Park, which includes over 52,000 hectares of pure nature.

The park is home to a broad diversity of animals, including kangaroos, emus, and numerous kinds of birds. Visitors can explore the park by automobile, or join a guided tour to learn more about the surrounding flora and animals.

For those interested in history, Shark Bay is also home to various historic landmarks, including the Old Pearler's Cemetery, which goes back to the 1800s. The region was formerly a centre for the pearling business, and tourists may learn about the history of the industry and the individuals who worked in it.

One of the most remarkable sights of Shark Bay is the stromatolites, which are regarded to be some of the oldest living fossils in the world. The stromatolites are generated by the proliferation of small microbes over thousands of years, and are found only in a few places in the globe. Visitors may observe the stromatolites up close in the Hamelin Pool Marine Nature Reserve.

Shark Bay

Monkey Mia Dolphin Resort

BEACHES AND SURFING SPOTS IN WESTERN AUSTRALIA

Western Australia is renowned for its beautiful coastline and pristine beaches that offer a wide range of surfing opportunities. The state's coastline spans over 12,000 kilometers, providing surfers with endless options to choose from.

Western Australia is also known for its consistent waves, crystal-clear waters, and uncrowded beaches, making it a surfer's paradise. Here are some top Beaches and surfing spots in Western Australia

Margaret River: Margaret River is a popular surfing destination located in the southwest region of Western Australia. It is home to some of the best surf breaks in the country, including Main Break, which is renowned for its powerful waves that can reach up to 20 feet high.

Yallingup: Yallingup is another popular surfing destination located in the Margaret River region. It is known for its consistent waves and uncrowded beaches, making it a great spot for surfers of all levels.

Rottnest Island: Rottnest Island is a small island located off the coast of Perth, Western Australia. It is known for its clear blue waters and excellent surfing conditions. Some of the best surf breaks on the island include Strickland Bay, Salmon Bay, and Stark Bay.

Scarborough Beach: Scarborough Beach is a popular beach located in the suburb of Scarborough in Perth. It is known for its consistent waves and is a great spot for beginner and intermediate surfers.

Trigg Beach: Trigg Beach is another popular beach located in Perth that is known for its consistent waves and long surf breaks. It is a great spot for intermediate and advanced surfers.

Esperance: Esperance is a town located in the southern region of Western Australia. It is known for its crystal-clear waters and uncrowded beaches, making it a great spot for surfers looking for a more secluded experience.

Apart from surfing, Western Australia also offers a range of other water sports, such as kiteboarding, windsurfing, and stand-up paddleboarding.

SHOPPING AND DINING IN WESTERN AUSTRALIA

Western Australia offers a wide range of shopping and dining experiences, from the trendy boutiques and high-end restaurants of Perth to the laid-back cafes and markets of the coastal towns. Here are some of the best places to shop and dine in Western Australia:

Perth City: As the largest city in Western Australia, Perth offers an array of shopping and dining options. Some of the top shopping destinations include the Murray Street Mall, Hay Street Mall, and the upscale King Street. For dining, there are plenty of options from high-end restaurants to casual cafes and bars.

Margaret River: Known for its wine region, Margaret River is also home to a variety of boutique shops and local markets.

The town center is lined with unique shops selling locally made products, as well as art galleries and souvenir stores. There are also many cafes and restaurants serving fresh and locally sourced cuisine.

Fremantle: This historic port town south of Perth is a popular destination for shopping and dining. The cobbled streets of the town center are lined with boutique shops, galleries, and markets selling everything from artisanal goods to vintage clothing.

The Fremantle Markets are a must-visit for their lively atmosphere and wide range of food and drink stalls.

Broome: This coastal town in the Kimberley region offers a unique shopping and dining experience. The town center is home to a variety of art galleries and shops selling handmade crafts, as well as specialty stores selling pearls and other local gems. There are also plenty of cafes and restaurants serving up fresh seafood and other local cuisine.

Rottnest Island: This popular holiday destination just off the coast of Perth is known for its stunning beaches and laid-back atmosphere. The island is also home to a variety of shops selling everything from beachwear to souvenirs, as well as cafes and restaurants serving up casual and family-friendly fare.

Cottesloe: This coastal suburb of Perth is home to one of the city's most popular beaches and a vibrant dining scene. There are plenty of cafes and restaurants along the main strip serving up fresh seafood and other local dishes, as well as boutique shops selling unique gifts and souvenirs.

WESTERN AUSTRALIA NIGHTLIFE

Western Australia has a vibrant nightlife with a diverse range of entertainment options available. Perth is the hub of nightlife in Western Australia, with numerous bars and nightclubs located in the central business district. One of the most popular areas for nightlife is Northbridge, which is home to a variety of bars, nightclubs, and live music venues. Here you can find everything from casual pubs to upscale cocktail bars.

Another popular nightlife destination in Western Australia is Fremantle, which is located south of Perth. This historic port city is home to a lively entertainment district with a wide range of bars and clubs. Fremantle is also known for its live music scene, with many venues featuring local and international musicians.

For those looking for a more laid-back evening, Western Australia also has many excellent restaurants and cafes. Perth has a thriving food scene with a wide range of cuisines on offer, including Asian, Mediterranean, and seafood.

Many of the city's restaurants are located in the central business district, but there are also many excellent options in the suburbs and surrounding areas.

Western Australia also has a thriving arts and cultural scene. There are numerous theaters, galleries, and performance venues located throughout the state, offering a diverse range of entertainment options.

CHAPTER SEVEN

SOUTH AUSTRALIA

South Australia is a state located in the southern central section of Australia. It is the fourth biggest state in the country and is surrounded by Western Australia to the west, the Northern Territory to the north, Queensland to the northeast, New South Wales to the east, Victoria to the southeast, and the Indian Ocean to the south.

The capital city of South Australia is Adelaide, which is also the sixth biggest city in Australia.

South Australia is noted for its distinctive scenery, diversified animals, and rich history. The state is home to numerous world-renowned wine areas, including the Barossa Valley and the Clare Valley, as well as scenic coastal villages, such as Victor Harbor and Robe.
The state is also home to some notable sights, including Kangaroo Island, the Flinders Ranges, and the Murray River.

South Australia has a rich history spanning back thousands of years, with the indigenous peoples being the first to inhabit the region. European colonization began in the early 19th century, with Adelaide being established in 1836.

The state had a vital part in the country's economic prosperity, with mining, agriculture, and manufacturing being prominent industries.

Today, South Australia is a dynamic and diversified state with a booming economy, a strong cultural scene, and a reputation for producing some of the greatest food and wine in the world.

With its breathtaking landscapes, rich cultural heritage, and warm residents, South Australia is a must-visit destination for tourists eager to discover the best that Australia has to offer.

TOP ATTRACTIONS IN SOUTH AUSTRALIA

South Australia is a state in the southern central part of Australia, known for its stunning landscapes, rich history, and vibrant culture. Some of the top attractions in South Australia include:

- **ADELAIDE**

Adelaide is the capital city of South Australia, and it is recognized for its superb food and wine scene, cultural events, and festivals, world-class galleries, and museums, as well as its gorgeous architecture.

The city is situated on the Torrens River and flanked by parklands, which makes it a perfect location for individuals who appreciate outdoor sports.

One of the most prominent sights in Adelaide is the Adelaide Oval, which is a world-renowned cricket venue that holds both cricket and Australian Rules Football (AFL) matches. The oval has a capacity of up to 50,000 people, and it is regarded one of the top stadiums in the world.

Another famous site in Adelaide is the Central Market, which is one of the largest undercover marketplaces in the Southern Hemisphere. The market offers a vast choice of fresh fruit, meats, seafood, and speciality delicacies from across the world.

For individuals interested in history, the South Australian Museum is a must-visit place. The museum is home to a wide collection of natural history and cultural relics, including an amazing collection of Aboriginal art and artifacts.

Other famous sites in Adelaide include the Botanic Gardens, the Art Gallery of South Australia, the Adelaide Zoo, and the South Australian Maritime Museum. The city also boasts a busy nighttime culture, with lots of pubs, restaurants, and nightclubs to satisfy all preferences.

- **THE ADELAIDE HILLS**

The Adelaide Hills is a scenic location located immediately east of Adelaide, the capital city of South Australia. It is a region noted for its natural beauty, attractive villages, and broad range of activities, making it a popular destination for visitors and locals alike.

One of the primary attractions of the Adelaide Hills is the gorgeous terrain. Visitors may explore the region's undulating hills, lush woods, and vineyards, which produce some of the country's finest wines.

The region is also home to several parks and reserves, like the Mount Lofty Botanic Garden and Belair National Park, where tourists may take in spectacular vistas and witness native animals.

In addition to natural beauty, the Adelaide Hills is also recognized for its rich cultural past. The region is home to a variety of ancient towns, such as Hahndorf, which was founded by German immigrants in the 19th century.

Visitors may explore Hahndorf's heritage buildings, boutique boutiques, and cafés, and learn about the town's unique history at the German Migration Museum.

Another major attraction in the Adelaide Hills is the food and wine scene. The region is home to a variety of award-winning vineyards, where tourists may experience some of the greatest wines in Australia.

The Adelaide Hills is also noted for its gourmet food, with many restaurants, cafés, and farmers' markets highlighting local goods.

For those seeking excitement, the Adelaide Hills provides a choice of sports such as cycling, hiking, and mountain riding. The location is also a famous site for hot air ballooning, with tourists able to take in panoramic views of the gorgeous environment from above.

- **THE BAROSSA VALLEY**

The Barossa Valley is a renowned wine-producing region located in South Australia, roughly 70 kilometers northeast of

Adelaide. It is home to some of the oldest vineyards in the world, going back to the mid-19th century when German farmers came in the region.

Today, the area is famous internationally for its award-winning wines, gourmet gastronomy, and gorgeous landscape.

The Barossa Valley is made up of various tiny communities, each with its distinct character and charm. Tanunda, Nuriootpa, and Angaston are the largest and most popular towns, although smaller towns like Lyndoch and Williamstown are also worth visiting.

The region's vineyards are mostly found on the valley level and the surrounding hills, having over 150 wineries to select from.

One of the greatest ways to see the Barossa Valley is on a wine tour. There are various tour companies available, giving guided tours of the vineyards and cellar doors, wine tastings, and gourmet culinary experiences. Many vineyards also provide lodging, ranging from modest bed & breakfasts to sophisticated resorts.

Apart from wine tasting, there are various more attractions to enjoy in the Barossa Valley. Visitors may luxuriate in the region's gourmet cuisine options, from handmade cheeses and chocolates to farm-fresh veggies and speciality meats. The Barossa Farmers Market, held every Saturday, is a must-visit for foodies.

For a sense of the region's history, tourists can travel to the Barossa Valley Museum or the Barossa Regional Gallery. The Whispering Wall at Barossa Reservoir is also a famous sight, where visitors may test the wall's unusual acoustic capabilities by whispering at one end and hearing the sound conveyed to the other end.

Outdoor lovers will appreciate exploring the region's gorgeous environment, with various hiking and cycling paths to pick from. The Barossa Trail is a popular alternative, offering 40 kilometers of picturesque cycling tracks through the vineyards and rolling hills.

For a more leisurely pace, guests can take a hot air balloon trip above the valley or enjoy a lovely drive through the countryside.

• KANGAROO ISLAND

Kangaroo Island is an island located off the coast of South Australia and is the third-largest island in Australia. The island is home to a rich assortment of species, magnificent beaches, and spectacular scenery, making it a popular destination for tourists. Here are some of the things that make Kangaroo Island a must-visit destination:

Wildlife: Kangaroo Island is home to a huge assortment of native creatures, many of which are not found anywhere else in the world. Visitors can spot kangaroos, wallabies, echidnas, and koalas, among others. Seal Bay Conservation Park is a must-visit, where tourists can get up close with a colony of endangered Australian sea lions.

Landscapes: Kangaroo Island features some of the most stunning landscapes in Australia, with rocky coastline, high cliffs, and clean beaches. Visitors may visit Flinders Chase National Park, which is home to the Remarkable Rocks and Admirals Arch, two of the island's most recognizable sights.

Food and Wine: The Barossa Valley may be more famous, but Kangaroo Island is also a fantastic destination for food and wine enthusiasts. The island is home to a selection of boutique wineries producing award-winning wines, as well as local manufacturers of artisan cheese, honey, and olive oil.

Adventure Activities: Visitors may experience a multitude of adventure activities on Kangaroo Island, including kayaking, fishing, and hiking.

The island also provides the option to swim with dolphins and seals or join a 4WD excursion to explore some of the island's more secluded parts.

Culture: Kangaroo Island has a rich indigenous history, and tourists may study the island's cultural legacy at the KI Cultural Centre in Kingscote.

- **FLINDERS RANGES**

Flinders Ranges is a picturesque mountain range in South Australia that is located around 400 kilometers to the north of Adelaide. It is the greatest mountain range in the state, and it runs across a distance of around 430 kilometers from Port Pirie in the south to Lake Callabonna in the north.

The Flinders Ranges is a popular location for outdoor enthusiasts, wildlife lovers, and people who wish to discover the breathtaking beauty of the Australian outback.

The Flinders Ranges is home to a variety of fauna, including kangaroos, wallabies, emus, and echidnas. There are also a variety of various bird species that may be spotted in the region, including wedge-tailed eagles, kookaburras, and parrots. The topography of the Flinders Ranges is characterized by rocky mountain ranges, deep gorges, and wide plains.

One of the most popular activities to undertake in the Flinders Ranges is hiking. There are several different hiking paths in the region, ranging from short walks to more demanding excursions that need a high degree of fitness.

The Heysen Trail is one of the most recognized hiking paths in the region, running over 1,200 kilometers from Cape Jervis to Parachilna Gorge. The path runs through some of the most stunning landscapes in South Australia, including the Flinders Ranges.

Visitors to the Flinders Ranges may also explore the area by automobile, with several beautiful routes that give spectacular views of the mountains, gorges, and plains. The drive from Port Augusta to Wilpena Pound is exceptionally scenic, and travelers may also see the ancient villages of Quorn and Hawker along the way.

Another popular pastime in the Flinders Ranges is animal spotting. Visitors may witness a number of various species in their native habitats, including kangaroos, wallabies, emus, and wedge-tailed eagles.

There are also numerous other conservation parks in the area, including the Flinders Ranges National Park, where visitors may learn about the flora and animals of the region.

- **LAKE EYRE**

Lake Eyre is a huge, salt-covered lake situated in the isolated area of South Australia. It is located in the lowest point of the Australian continent and is one of the most distinctive natural landmarks in the world. The lake is really a collection of numerous smaller lakes, including Lake Eyre South, Lake Eyre North, and Lake Eyre itself.

Lake Eyre is one of the biggest salt lakes in the world and has remained dry for much of its life. However, when it does receive rain, it becomes a wonderful natural marvel that attracts tourists from all over the world.

The lake's water originates from many rivers, including the Warburton, Neales, and Cooper Creek, which only flow into the lake following significant rains.

The lake has a unique environment that supports a varied range of flora and wildlife. When the lake fills with water, it provides a breeding site for thousands of birds, including pelicans, swans, and ducks. The lake also supports a number of fish species, including golden perch, catfish, and Murray cod.

Lake Eyre is also a key cultural place for the local Indigenous people, who have inhabited the region for thousands of years. The lake is said to be the home of the Kumudra, a strong snake that is claimed to govern the water and the seasons.

Visitors to Lake Eyre may explore the lake's beautiful sceneries by foot, automobile, or plane. There are various vantage locations that give panoramic views of the lake and its surrounds. The greatest time to see the lake is after heavy rains when it is at its most magnificent.

In addition to the lake itself, there are various additional attractions in the Lake Eyre region, including the Oodnadatta Track, a historic 615-kilometer trail that passes through the heart of the Australian outback. The road travels through numerous isolated settlements and gives tourists an opportunity to discover the region's distinctive culture and traditions.

- **COORONG NATIONAL PARK**

Coorong National Park is a protected region located in South Australia, roughly 150 kilometers southeast of Adelaide. The park was founded in 1966 and encompasses an area of roughly 50,000 hectares. The park is named after a network of interconnecting coastal lagoons that span for over 100 kilometers along the southeast coast of South Australia. The Coorong is one of Australia's most significant wetland ecosystems and is widely known for its value as a refuge for migrating birds.

The Coorong National Park is highlighted by its spectacular coastline beauty, diversified flora and wildlife, and distinct cultural history. The park is home to a diversity of distinct habitats, including salt marshes, mudflats, samphire flats, and coastal dunes.

The area is rich in biodiversity and supports a variety of plant and animal species, including rare and endangered species such as the orange-bellied parrot and the southern right whale.

One of the most popular activities at the Coorong National Park is bird viewing. The park is home to around 240 kinds of birds, including pelicans, terns, gulls, and cormorants. The park also supports a considerable population of migratory waders, who migrate to the Coorong from as far away as the Arctic Circle.

The Coorong National Park is also home to a variety of cultural sites that highlight the park's Aboriginal past. The Ngarrindjeri people have lived in the Coorong region for thousands of years and have a profound spiritual connection to the land and waters.

Other popular activities in the Coorong National Park include fishing, kayaking, and camping. The park offers a variety of campsites that offer minimal services, including bathrooms and fire pits.

The park is also home to a variety of walking paths that allow visitors to experience the area's spectacular coastline environment and distinctive flora and wildlife.

- **CLARE VALLEY**

Clare Valley is a scenic valley located in the Mid North of South Australia, about 136 kilometers from Adelaide. This picturesque valley is famous for its vineyards, gorgeous landscapes, ancient villages, and pleasant residents.

The Clare Valley is one of Australia's oldest wine districts, having a wine-making tradition that stretches back to the 1840s. The valley is home to some of the most noteworthy wine-producing locations in the country and is recognized for its world-class Riesling.

The Clare Valley's picturesque terrain boasts rolling hills, gorgeous vineyards, and tiny rural villages. It is the perfect spot to escape the hustle and bustle of the city and immerse yourself in nature.

Wine aficionados will be spoiled for choice in the Clare Valley, which offers more than 40 cellar doors, each offering a distinct wine-tasting experience. The valley's vineyards are famed for their world-class Rieslings, but tourists may also experience a broad selection of other varietals, including Shiraz, Cabernet Sauvignon, and Grenache.

Aside from wine tasting, there are lots of other things to see and do in the Clare Valley. Visitors may discover the region's rich history by visiting the ancient towns of Burra, Mintaro, and Auburn, which have well maintained buildings and historic sites.

The valley is also home to a selection of art galleries, antique stores, and boutique shops, making it the perfect place for a little of shopping therapy.

Nature enthusiasts will appreciate the Clare Valley's spectacular natural surroundings, which includes the Spring Gully Conservation Park, Sevenhill Conservation Park, and the Clare Valley Golf Course. Visitors may enjoy a leisurely walk around the valley's lovely landscape or explore one of the many hiking routes that snake through the region's challenging terrain.

The Clare Valley is also home to a number of wonderful restaurants, cafés, and diners. Visitors may indulge in gourmet meals, local vegetables, and world-class wines at one of the valley's numerous award-winning restaurants or experience fresh produce at one of the local markets.

- **WILPENA POUND**

Wilpena Pound is a natural amphitheater found in the Flinders Ranges area of South Australia. It is a beautiful landmark that has been a cultural and spiritual place for the Adnyamathanha people for thousands of years.

The Pound is a massive basin-like formation, generally round in shape, with steep sides that reach to almost 1,000 meters high. The whole Pound spans an area of roughly 80 square kilometers and is bordered by high mountains and deep canyons.

One of the greatest ways to explore Wilpena Pound is via hiking. There are various hiking paths in the region, ranging from short walks to more demanding hikes.

The Wilpena Pound hike is a popular one, affording spectacular views of the Pound from different viewpoints. The hike is roughly 12 kilometers long and takes around five hours to finish. The route winds through the Pound's core basin and gives beautiful views of the surrounding mountains, valleys, and rock formations.

Another popular activity in Wilpena Pound is scenic flying. There are various firms that provide beautiful flights over the Pound and neighboring areas. These flights provide a unique viewpoint of the Pound, and also offer spectacular views of the Flinders Ranges and the surrounding countryside.

The region is also rich in wildlife, with kangaroos, emus, and wallabies commonly observed in the surrounding areas. There are also numerous bird species that make the region home, including wedge-tailed eagles, kookaburras, and galahs.

Visitors may also learn about the Adnyamathanha people's culture and history by taking a guided tour of the region. The excursions are guided by local indigenous guides who share their expertise and stories about the area's history and significance.

Accommodation choices in the region range from camping and caravanning to luxury hotels and resorts. The Wilpena Pound Resort is a popular alternative, offering a number of lodging options and services, including a restaurant, bar, and swimming pool.

• PORT LINCOLN

Port Lincoln is a seaside town located on the Eyre Peninsula in South Australia. It is recognized for its magnificent surroundings, recreational activities, and superb seafood. Here are some of the things to see and do in Port Lincoln:

Shark Cage Diving: Port Lincoln is one of the few spots in the world where you can go cage diving with great white sharks. Adventure lovers may embark on a day excursion to Neptune Island to observe these remarkable creatures up up and personal.

Fishing: Port Lincoln is also recognized as the seafood capital of Australia. Visitors may embark on a fishing trip to capture tuna, snapper, and kingfish. You may also try the freshest fish at the local eateries.

Wildlife Experiences: Visitors may also enjoy a tour of the Mikkira Station, which is home to a colony of wild koalas. You may also take a tour to Glen-Forest Tourist Park to view kangaroos, wallabies, and emus.

Lincoln National Park: The park is located on the southern extremity of the Eyre Peninsula and offers spectacular coastline scenery, bushwalking paths, and camping options. Visitors may also admire the stunning views from the Stamford Hill Lookout.

Coffin Bay National Park: This park is located just north of Port Lincoln and features beautiful beaches, sand dunes, and a picturesque shoreline. Visitors may also take a boat cruise to view the oyster farms in the vicinity.

Whalers Way: This is a magnificent road that takes you down the coast of the Eyre Peninsula. Visitors may witness spectacular rock formations, isolated beaches, and animals such as seals and dolphins.

Arts & cultural: Port Lincoln also boasts a flourishing arts and cultural scene. Visitors may tour the Nautilus Arts Centre and the Port Lincoln Civic Hall, which highlight local artists and entertainment.

Local products: Visitors may also experience the local products, including the famed Port Lincoln oysters, wines from the Eyre Peninsula, and organic vegetables and fruits from the local farmers' market.

BEST PLACES TO SHOP AND DINE IN SOUTH AUSTRALIA

South Australia provides a range of alternatives for shopping and dining, ranging from local food to upscale dining experiences.

One of the biggest shopping places in South Australia is Rundle Mall in Adelaide. This pedestrian street mall is loaded with boutique shops, department stores, and renowned brands. Here, tourists may discover anything from clothes and accessories to cosmetic items and household goods. Another famous shopping area is the Adelaide Central Market, where tourists can explore a lively indoor market full with local vegetables, artisanal items, and more.

For those searching for a fine dining experience, South Australia boasts numerous award-winning restaurants. Adelaide is home to numerous Michelin-starred restaurants, including Orana and The Cube.

These restaurants provide a distinct culinary experience, employing locally sourced ingredients to produce inventive meals. Other popular fine dining alternatives include Penfolds Magill Estate Restaurant, The Salopian Inn in McLaren Vale, and Appellation in the Barossa Valley.

In addition to exquisite dining, South Australia is famed for its vineyards and wine regions, including the Barossa Valley, McLaren Vale, and the Clare Valley. These areas provide cellar door tastings and tours, as well as gourmet dining experiences.

For those searching for a more informal eating experience, South Australia also boasts a number of alternatives, from food trucks to classic pubs.

The beachfront village of Port Lincoln is famed for its fresh seafood, with various local seafood restaurants serving a range of meals, including oysters, scallops, and tuna. In Adelaide, the

Central Market provides a range of street food alternatives, from Asian cuisine to local products.

SOUTH AUSTRALIA NIGHTLIFE

South Australia is recognized for its active nightlife, offering a variety of options ranging from fashionable pubs and nightclubs to live music venues and eateries. Whether you are in Adelaide, the state capital, or in one of the rural cities, there are plenty of alternatives to select from.

Adelaide is home to some of the top nightlife venues in South Australia. The city's dynamic bar culture appeals to a wide range of interests and prices, with everything from sophisticated rooftop bars to intimate wine bars and craft beer pubs.

Rundle Street is one of the city's primary nightlife areas, offering a broad assortment of pubs and clubs that stay up late into the night. Peel Street and Leigh Street are other popular areas for cocktails and late-night meals.

Live music is also a key element of Adelaide's nightlife, with several venues featuring local and international acts throughout the year. Venues such as The Gov, Thebarton Theatre, and Adelaide Entertainment Centre are renowned for live music performances.

For those seeking for something more relaxed, Adelaide also boasts a choice of wine bars and restaurants that offer an intimate ambiance for a night out. The city is recognized for its local wine areas, and many taverns and restaurants offer a vast range of wines from around South Australia.

Outside of Adelaide, there are lots of opportunities for nightlife in the smaller centers. Mount Gambier, for example, has a busy bar culture, with various establishments presenting live music and events. Port Lincoln, located on the Eyre Peninsula, also features a choice of bars and taverns that stay open late.

CHAPTER EIGHT

TASMANIA

Tasmania is a tiny island state located south of mainland Australia. It is noted for its natural beauty, with rough beaches, lush forests, and alpine wilderness regions.

The island state is also home to a rich historical and cultural legacy, with indigenous Tasmanians having occupied the island for over 35,000 years until the entrance of European immigrants in the 19th century.

Today, Tasmania is a popular tourist destination, giving tourists a unique combination of natural beauty, cultural attractions, and gourmet cuisine and wine.

Tasmania is a very tiny state, with a land area of slightly over 68,000 square kilometers. It is home to a population of roughly 540,000 people, with the bulk of citizens living in the capital city of Hobart or in the bigger rural communities of Launceston and Devonport.

Despite its tiny size, Tasmania offers visitors a multitude of activities, ranging from historic sites and cultural encounters to outdoor excursions and gastronomic pleasures.

TOP ATTRACTIONS IN TASMANIA

Tasmania, the island state of Australia, is noted for its rough natural beauty, historic landmarks, and rich fauna. Here are some of the best attractions in Tasmania:

FREYCINET NATIONAL PARK: This national park is home to spectacular natural landscapes including mountains, beaches, and turquoise bays. Visitors may take a trek to the top of Wineglass Bay overlook, explore the Hazards Beach, and observe animals such as wallabies and echidnas.

CRADLE MOUNTAIN-LAKE ST. CLAIR NATIONAL PARK: This park is one of Tasmania's most popular attractions, recognized for its gorgeous vistas and great hiking paths. The park is home to Cradle Mountain, a high peak surrounded by glacial lakes and ancient woods.

PORT ARTHUR HISTORIC SITE: This former convict colony is now a UNESCO World Heritage Site and one of Tasmania's most famous tourist sites. Visitors may explore the ruins of the former jail, learn about Tasmania's colonial history, and enjoy a ghost tour at night.

SALAMANCA MARKET: This outdoor market in Hobart is a must-visit for shopping and dining. Visitors may peruse stalls selling handcrafted goods, local vegetables, and artisanal food and drink, while enjoying live music and street entertainment.

MONA (MUSEUM OF OLD AND NEW ART): This museum is one of the most distinctive art museums in the world, noted for its provocative and controversial displays. The museum also has a vineyard, brewery, and restaurant, making it a perfect visit for food and wine aficionados.

BRUNY ISLAND: This island off the coast of Tasmania is a delight for environment enthusiasts, with rich animals, gorgeous hiking paths, and wonderful beaches. Visitors may also take a tour of the Bruny Island Lighthouse or enjoy local goods at the Bruny Island Cheese Company.

TAMAR VALLEY: This gorgeous region in northern Tasmania is recognized for its vineyards, breweries, and cideries, as well as its magnificent vistas. Visitors may take a wine tour, go kayaking on the Tamar River, or see ancient cities such as Launceston and George Town.

MOUNT WELLINGTON: This summit above Hobart gives excellent views of the city and surrounding beaches. Visitors may trek to the peak or take a beautiful drive, and enjoy panoramic views from the observation deck.

HASTINGS TUNNELS & THERMAL SPRINGS: This natural site in southern Tasmania contains a series of tunnels filled with magnificent formations, as well as a thermal spring that's great for bathing. Visitors may enjoy a guided tour of the caverns or rest in the warm water of the pool.

MARIA ISLAND: This island off the east coast of Tasmania is a protected national park famed for its unspoilt scenery and plentiful fauna. Visitors may take a guided tour, go hiking or cycling, or simply enjoy the beaches and picturesque scenery.

HIKING AND NATURE IN TASMANIA

Tasmania is an island state of Australia that is recognized for its magnificent scenery, rough terrain, and unusual animals. The state is a hiker's dream, with hundreds of hiking paths that take tourists through ancient rainforests, along rocky coasts, and up to high mountain summits.

The island is also home to a number of national parks and reserves, which give tourists an opportunity to explore some of the most pristine wilderness places in the world.

Cradle Mountain is one of Tasmania's most renowned hiking sites. The peak is part of the Cradle peak-Lake St Clair National Park, which is a World Heritage Area owing to its exceptional natural beauty and cultural value.

There are a multitude of hiking paths that carry tourists through the park, ranging from modest walks to more strenuous multi-day excursions. The Overland Track is one of the most popular hiking tracks in the park, bringing tourists on a six-day trip through some of Tasmania's most magnificent wilderness areas.

The Tasman Peninsula is another famous hiking area in Tasmania. The peninsula is located on the eastern coast of the state, and is home to a variety of hiking routes that lead tourists through spectacular coastal scenery and through historic sights such as the Port Arthur penal colony.

The Three Capes Track is one of the most popular hiking pathways on the peninsula, bringing visitors on a four-day trek through some of the most magnificent coastal scenery in Tasmania.

Tasmania is also home to a variety of world-renowned wilderness regions, including the Southwest National Park and the Franklin-Gordon Wild Rivers National Park. These parks are home to some of the most spectacular scenery in Australia, including old rainforests, steep mountains, and wild rivers.

Visitors to these parks can explore the wilderness on foot, by boat, or by helicopter, depending on their interests and physical levels.

The state is home to a variety of species that are found nowhere else in the world, including the Tasmanian devil, the eastern quoll, and the Tasmanian pademelon.

Visitors can join guided excursions to observe these species in their natural environment, or visit wildlife sanctuaries and parks to learn more about their biology and conservation status.

BEST PLACES TO SHOP AND DINE IN TASMANIA

Tasmania may be recognized for its natural beauty, but it also has lots to offer in terms of shopping and dining. From locally crafted artisanal items to fresh seafood, there's something for everyone in Tasmania. Here are some of the top locations to shop and dine in Tasmania:

Salamanca Market: Located in Hobart, the Salamanca Market is one of Tasmania's most famous shopping attractions. The market takes place every Saturday and contains over 300 vendors offering anything from local arts and crafts to fresh fruit.

Farm Gate Market: Another Hobart staple, the Farm Gate Market is a Sunday market that focuses on local vegetables. Here you may get fresh fruits and vegetables, meat, fish, baked products, and more.

Providore Place: This indoor market in Devonport contains a variety of local food and drink businesses, including a cheese shop, a fish market, and a craft brewery.

Cat & Fiddle Arcade: Located downtown Hobart, the Cat and Fiddle Arcade is home to a range of specialized stores selling anything from vintage books to handcrafted chocolates.

Brooke Street Pier: This seaside retail and eating sector in Hobart provides a range of alternatives, including seafood restaurants, cafés, and craft stores.

Josef Chromy Wines: This vineyard near Launceston provides wine tastings and a fine dining restaurant, emphasizing local vegetables and seafood.

Stillwater: Located in Launceston, Stillwater is a fine dining restaurant that specializes on modern Australian cuisine, incorporating local Tasmanian ingredients.

Franklin: This Hobart restaurant is noted for its unique spin on classic cuisine, with a rotating menu that reflects the seasonal availability of local vegetables.

The Agrarian Kitchen Eatery: Located in New Norfolk, The Agrarian Kitchen Eatery serves up substantial, rustic cuisine prepared with locally sourced ingredients.

Mures: This Hobart seafood tradition contains a restaurant, fishmonger, and takeout fish and chips store, all exhibiting the best Tasmanian seafood.

TASMANIA NIGHTLIFE

Tasmania may be a small island state, but it still provides plenty of alternatives for those seeking for a night out. Whether you're wanting a quiet drink with friends, a night of live music, or some excellent food, Tasmania has plenty to offer.

Hobart, the capital city of Tasmania, boasts a busy nightlife scene. Salamanca Place is a popular place for bars and pubs, offering a wide range of alternatives from casual pubs to cocktail bars.

The strip is also home to some of Hobart's greatest eateries, making it a popular destination for foodies. Another popular place is the North Hobart strip, which includes a lot of pubs and restaurants with a more alternative atmosphere.

Launceston, Tasmania's second-largest city, also boasts a busy nightlife scene. The city features a variety of bars, pubs, and clubs, featuring a mix of live music, DJs, and karaoke.

For those searching for something more refined, the city boasts a variety of cocktail bars and wine bars, providing a selection of local and foreign drinks.

Tasmania's smaller towns also have their own unique nightlife. For example, the town of Burnie on the north coast boasts a variety of pubs and clubs, as well as the Burnie Arts and Function Centre, which organizes regular performances by local and visiting artists.

In addition to bars and pubs, Tasmania also boasts a variety of events and festivals throughout the year that provide an opportunity to enjoy the local nightlife. These include the Dark Mofo festival in Hobart, which offers a mix of music, art, and cultural activities, and the Taste of Tasmania festival, which promotes the state's greatest cuisine and wine.

CHAPTER NINE

PRACTICAL INFORMATION AND RESOURCES

Some of the various tools and sources that visitors can use to plan and make the most of their trip to Australia includes:

- **TRAVEL DOCUMENTS**

Travel documents are necessary for entrance into Australia, and the type of document needed varies on the purpose and length of your stay. The following are some of the most popular travel papers necessary to visit Australia:

Passport: All passengers, including minors, must have a valid passport to enter Australia. The passport must be valid for at least six months beyond the estimated duration of stay in Australia.

Visa: Depending on the traveler's nationality and the purpose of the visit, a visa may be required to enter Australia. There are several sorts of visas available, including tourist visas, working holiday visas, and student visas.

It is vital to consult the Australian Government's Department of Home Affairs website to discover which sort of visa is required for your travel.

Electronic Travel Authority (ETA): An ETA is an electronically stored permission that permits qualifying passport holders to enter and remain in Australia for up to three months. ETA holders can visit Australia as many times as they like throughout the validity term, which is normally 12 months.

Visitor Visa: A visitor visa is for persons who intend to visit Australia for tourism, visiting family or friends, or for business purposes. The visiting visa enables stays of up to three, six, or 12 months, depending on the visa category.

eVisitor: The eVisitor is an electronic visa offered to passport holders from qualifying European nations. This visa enables stays of up to three months in Australia for vacation, visiting family or friends, or for business activities.

Medical Treatment Visa: The medical treatment visa is for persons who need medical care in Australia that is not accessible in their native country. This visa enables stays of up to three months.

It is crucial to remember that admission criteria might change at any moment, therefore it is necessary to check the Australian Government's Department of Home Affairs website for the latest information. It is suggested that tourists apply for their visa well in advance of their scheduled travel date, as processing periods might vary.

● CURRENCY

Currency in Australia is the Australian dollar (AUD). It is abbreviated with the sign "$" or occasionally "A$" to differentiate it from other currencies utilizing the dollar symbol. The Australian dollar is a decimal currency, with one dollar consisting of 100 cents.

Banknotes come in denominations of $5, $10, $20, $50, and $100. Coins come in denominations of 5c, 10c, 20c, 50c, $1, and $2. The notes are constructed of polymer and are quite durable, while the coins are made of a mix of metals.

Australia has a well-developed financial system, with ATMs extensively distributed across the country. Credit cards are frequently accepted, including Visa, Mastercard, and American Express. Many businesses and restaurants also accept digital wallets such as Apple Pay and Google Pay.

It's important to know that currency conversion rates can fluctuate constantly, so it's always a good idea to check current prices before flying to Australia. Additionally, visitors should be aware of any costs linked with currency conversion or overseas transactions to prevent any surprise expenditures.

When going to Australia, it's advisable to pack a combination of cash and credit cards, and to tell your bank or credit card provider of your vacation intentions to avoid any complications with fraud protection measures.

- **HEALTH AND SAFETY**

Health and safety are crucial considerations for every trip to Australia. It is crucial to take required steps to guarantee a safe and healthy travel.

One of the largest health risks in Australia is sun exposure. The nation is known for its long, hot summers and strong UV levels, therefore it is necessary to protect your skin from the sun. Use a high SPF sunscreen, wear a hat and sunglasses, and seek shade during the warmest times of the day.

Another health risk in Australia is the prevalence of poisonous species such as snakes, spiders, and jellyfish. Be cautious when exploring natural regions and heed the advice of local experts.

It is also necessary to be mindful of water safety. Australia offers some of the world's most beautiful beaches, yet they may be dangerous owing to powerful currents and rips. Always swim between the flags and follow the instructions of lifeguards.

Travelers should also be wary of the possibility of bushfires, particularly during the summer months. Check local fire risk ratings and follow the advice of local authorities.

Australia offers a good quality of healthcare, but it is necessary to have appropriate travel insurance to cover any unforeseen medical bills. It is also a good idea to investigate any essential vaccines or prescriptions for your trip.

As with any vacation, it is vital to follow basic safety precautions. Keep valuables protected, remain mindful of your surroundings, and observe local laws and traditions.

- **TRANSPORTATION**

Transportation in Australia is diversified, efficient and typically dependable. Whether you are going inside a city, across cities or across the nation, there are various alternatives to select from.

Air Travel: Air travel is the most popular means of transportation over vast distances inside Australia. Major cities and outlying areas are supplied by a network of airlines. The two major airlines are Qantas and Virgin Australia. Other airlines that operate inside the nation include Jetstar, Tigerair and Rex Airlines. Air travel is fast, safe and efficient, making it the preferred means of transportation for business and leisure tourists.

Train Travel: Train travel is a popular method to visit the nation and gives a unique approach to observe the Australian countryside. The two largest railway operators in Australia are Great Southern Railways and Queensland Railways. There are various long-distance rail services, including the Indian Pacific, The Ghan, and the Spirit of Queensland.

Bus Travel: Bus travel is a common means of transportation for short to medium distances, particularly in regional locations. Greyhound Australia is the largest bus operator in Australia, delivering services to major cities and outlying locations. Other bus companies include Premier Motor Service, Firefly Express, and Murrays.

Car hiring: Car hiring is a popular alternative for those who wish to see Australia at their own leisure. There are various automobile rental businesses, including Avis, Budget, Europcar, Hertz and Thrifty. Renting a car in Australia is reasonably affordable and allows the option to go at your own speed.

Taxis and Ride-sharing: Taxis and ride-sharing services such as Uber are extensively accessible in Australia. Taxis can be hailed from the street or hired in advance. Ride-sharing services may be booked via a smartphone app.

Ferries: Ferries are a popular means of transportation for people who want to see the islands of Australia. There are various ferry providers, including Sealink, Rottnest Express and Spirit of Tasmania.

Cycling: Cycling is a common means of transportation in metropolitan areas and is a terrific way to explore the cities. Many cities provide bike rental programs and designated bike lanes.

Transportation in Australia is diversified and efficient. With various alternatives to select from, tourists may explore the nation at their own pace and convenience.

- **ACCOMMODATION**

Travelers can choose from a variety of lodging alternatives in Australia. There is lodging to suit every taste and budget, ranging from affordable hostels to opulent resorts.

Hotels and Resorts: In Australia, hotels and resorts are the most often used kind of lodging. From major chains to little inns, they come in various kinds and sizes.

Depending on the location and amount of luxury, costs might vary substantially. In Australia, some of the most well-known hotel chains include Accor, Hilton, Marriott, and InterContinental.

Holiday Parks: In Australia, holiday parks are a common kind of lodging. They often provide a variety of lodging alternatives, including cabins, RV parks, and campsites, and are situated in picturesque regions. There are amenities including swimming pools, playgrounds, and BBQ areas at many vacation parks.

Hostels: For those on a tight budget, hostels are an excellent choice. They are a fantastic opportunity to meet other travelers and provide shared dorms or private rooms. Additionally, many hostels have social spaces and community kitchens.

Airbnb: In Australia, Airbnb is a growingly well-liked lodging choice. Travelers can stay in distinctive and regional accommodations including apartments, homes, and even boats. Depending on the location and amount of luxury, costs might vary substantially.

Farm Stays: Australia offers a distinctive form of lodging in the form of farm stays. They enable visitors to get a taste of farm life and take part in tasks like egg collection and animal feeding. Farm stays often offer a tranquil and quiet break and are found in rural settings.

Camping is a well-liked kind of lodging for tourists who wish to experience Australia's breathtaking natural beauty. There are several camping possibilities, ranging from cost-free campgrounds to upscale camping excursions. National parks, beaches, and rural regions are a few of Australia's most well-liked camping spots.

• COMMUNICATION

Visitors shouldn't have any problem remaining connected when traveling in Australia because the country boasts a cutting-edge and effective communications infrastructure. Telstra, Optus, and Vodafone are the major telecommunications companies in the nation.

Australia has a large population of mobile phone users, and tourists may buy prepaid SIM cards from these carriers in the majority of retail locations, including airports, convenience stores, and electronics stores. Depending on the provider, the quantity of data, and the calling time included, different cards have different prices.

In Australia, Wi-Fi is also readily accessible, with the majority of hotels, cafés, and restaurants providing free or inexpensive internet access. There is free Wi-Fi available in many public locations, including libraries and transportation hubs.

International travelers should be aware that mobile phone roaming costs might be high. It is advised that travelers speak with their carrier to confirm the prices of international roaming before leaving for Australia.

As with any new place you visit, it's crucial to pay attention to your surroundings and exercise the necessary prudence when using technological gadgets. Visitors should use caution when using their devices in congested locations and should refrain from doing so while walking or operating a motor vehicle.

You should also take precautions to protect your equipment and personal information from theft and be aware of the possibility of theft.

• BEST TIME TO VISIT AUSTRALIA

The ideal time to visit Australia relies on a number of factors, including personal preferences, financial constraints, and planned activities. Australia is a large country with a diverse climate. But generally speaking, the shoulder season—that is, the time between the high and low seasons—is the ideal time for travelers to visit Australia.

Australia's summer, which lasts from December to February, is known as the high season. The majority of tourist destinations are packed during this time, and lodging, travel, and tour costs are expensive. However, the summer season is ideal for water sports including swimming, surfing, and snorkeling as well as beachgoers.

Australia's winter, which lasts from June through August, is known as the low season. The weather is chilly at this time of year, making several tourist sites, especially outdoor activities, inaccessible. The greatest time to go, however, is for those on a tight budget because lodging, travel, and tour costs are all quite inexpensive.

March through May and September through November are considered the shoulder seasons. The weather is pleasant, there are less crowds, and costs are reduced during this season. For those who want to explore the outdoors, animals, and unspoiled beauty of the nation, this is the perfect time to travel. The big cities are also fantastic times to visit because there are so many festivals and events going on at this time.

Australia is a big country, and the weather varies depending on where you are in the country. For instance, the tropical north has wet and dry seasons, respectively, from November to April and May to October.

CONCLUSION

Australia is a land of diverse experiences, from its rugged outback to its pristine beaches, vibrant cities, and rich cultural heritage. This travel guide has provided a comprehensive overview of the country's top attractions, outdoor activities, cultural experiences, dining, nightlife, accommodations, transportation, and practical information. You should plan your trip carefully, taking into account the best time to visit, travel documents, currency, health and safety considerations, and communication options. With the right preparation and a spirit of adventure, you are sure to have an unforgettable experience that will leave you with cherished memories for a lifetime on your trip to Australia.

Printed in Great Britain
by Amazon

56842246R00155